HAROLD

PROLOGUE BY

Victorious Warfare

Discovering your Rightful
Place in God's Kingdom

Most Bible quotations are taken from the New American Standard Bible, (Bible Master for Windows, Version 1.03, Copyright © 1989–1994, The Lockman Foundation, P.O. Box 2279, La Habra, CA 90631). Used with permission.

Other versions used are: Revised Standard Version (RSV).

(THE HOLY BIBLE: REVISED STANDARD VERSION. Copyright © 1946, 1952, 1973 by National Council of Churches of Christ. All rights reserved.) Used with permission.

21st Century King James Version (Online Bible, Version 7.00-C/WIN 32, June 2, 1997, Copyright © 1997, Timnathserah Inc., Winterbourne, Ontario, Canada, NOB 2V0). Used with permission.

The Holy Bible, New King James Version (NKJV), (Thomas Nelson Publishers, Copyright © 1982. Used with permission.)

New International Version (NIV), (The Holy Bible, New International Version ® Copyright © 1973, 1978, 1984 by International Bible Society. Used with permission.)

Library of Congress Cataloging-in-Publication Data

Caballeros, Harold.
    [De victoria en victoria. English]
    Victorious warfare: discovering your rightful place in God's kingdom / Harold Caballeros.
      p. cm.
    ISBN 0-7852-4605-3
    1. Spiritual warfare. I. Title.
    BV4509.5 . C3 2001
    235'.4—dc21
                                     00-053711
                                          CIP

Printed in the United States of America

1 2 3 4 5 6 — 06 05 04 03 02 01

Dedication

I dedicate this book, with great love, to my parents. Their leading has been a lighthouse every day of my life. I am grateful for their love, inspiration, and continual support. Above all, I am grateful because they taught me the concept of unconditional love.

Table of Contents

Prologue

I am persuaded this book will be a great blessing to the church of the Lord Jesus Christ throughout the world. Dr. Harold Caballeros and I have been friends for many years. I have seen him minister, I have been in his church in Guatemala, and I have invited him to speak to the pastors in my crusades; his teachings have left eternal imprints in the hearts of the ones who hear them. We have spoken for long periods of time, I have seen his heart, and one thing I know is that the hand of the Lord is upon him.

The teaching you will receive in these pages is not simple theory, or an essay to find a magical solution. I always say that what is not lived should not be taught. The book you hold in your hands has years of ministry, dealings of the Lord and personal experiences.

This book is the result of:

1. The revelation of God to a pastor who is sincerely involved in the extension of the kingdom of God.

2. It is the systematic study of a man who does not rest until the changes produced when the message of the gospel reaches the communities are seen.

3. The passion of an apostle who has practiced, in his church, the principles he mentions in this book, and has planted

them in many parts of the world to reap hundreds of transformed ministers and churches.

I like this book because its pages carry the burden of the Lord Jesus Christ for lost souls; they have the same mind by which the Son of God came "to seek and to save that which was lost."

I like this book because it contains the strategies of spiritual warfare, but is not centered in them, or prayer or spiritual mapping. Spiritual warfare is presented here as an effective tool to conquer people and nations for Jesus Christ. It has the potential to produce an effect in heaven that is tangible and visible on earth.

This book shows the confrontation of powers from a sound biblical basis—not underestimated or overemphasized—presented in its right perspective to face and overcome as we take hold of what the Lord has provided.

As an evangelist, I have always been worried about new converts. This book gives us an answer on how to disciple and educate them so that they become involved in the place and task of the body of Christ.

It is a privilege for me to recommend *From Victory to Victory* to all the Christians in the world who have a burden to conquer the nations. I know that the book and its author are instruments of the Holy Spirit, chosen to fulfill His perfect plan until the Master returns.

My prayer is that God speaks to you as you walk through this writing.

—CARLOS ALBERTO ANNACONDIA
Buenos Aires, Argentina

Preface

The subject of spiritual warfare is biblical and is a genuine and important biblical theme. Nevertheless, just as has happened with other messages God has given to His Church, this subject is also liable to be taken to extremes. *We have witnessed some of those extremes but we also know that the spiritual warfare movement has now reached a level of maturity and recognition within the Body of Christ.*

I consider spiritual warfare to be a tool given by God for effective evangelism, revival, and the transformation of our society.

The people who know me have asked more than once why I waited so long to publish this book. *Personally, it was absolutely necessary to know that what we have preached generated measurable results. The years that have passed have been very special for the congregation I pastor. Throughout this time, we have learned many things. Most importantly, we have put them into practice and witnessed the power of God.* Today, we feel at ease presenting our contribution to the Church in the great task of evangelizing the world.

From a local church perspective, our description of the topic will be balanced and practical, and above all, continually supported by the Word of God. Our compass will be Matthew 13:23, "this is the man who hears the word and understands it; who indeed bears fruit, and brings forth, some a *hundredfold, some sixty, and some thirty."*

Before starting, let me express my gratitude to all the members of the El Shaddai congregation. Without their unconditional support, many of the things you are about to read simply would not have been possible. A million thanks to Cecilia, my wife, for being the source of encouragement for this project, and thank you, thank you very much to Ana Maria Fernandez, my secretary, and her daughters Karla and Ana Paola, for working again and again on the manuscript. Thank you.

—HAROLD CABALLEROS

Introduction

Due to the unique relationship established between the writer and the reader of a book, today we have the opportunity of launching on a journey that will take us through the holy Scriptures. It will take us to the heavens and the earth. It will transport us to a world of ideas and concepts that we possibly had not even examined. Above all, it will introduce us to everyday reality viewed from a different perspective. I can assure you that your focus in regards to evangelism will drastically change. Even the general idea that we have about Christian life will change when the Lord reveals His eternal purposes for the Church to our hearts. Truthfully, this book constitutes a monument to the love of God and to His unfathomable mercy in letting us know the revelation of what it means to be His "co-laborers."

I have written this book after many years of studying the subject of spiritual warfare. I have spent many hours studying, teaching, and practicing the principles you will find in these pages. I have witnessed, with the congregation I pastor, great miracles of God as a direct result of spiritual warfare. As I will show you further ahead, I have seen God perform the miracle of taking an entire city, and totally transforming it, through the application of these principles. I will quote the example of Almolonga, the "Miracle City," as a case study that has become a model of what warfare prayer can do in a territory when the Church gets into action. I have come to understand that spiritual warfare is a key element if revival is to come. I have proven that spiritual warfare can produce in a local church the results that every pastor desires. While I write these lines, our local church has an average of two hundred persons born again every week.

My personal experience shows that it is necessary to simultaneously do spiritual battle on three levels, as defined by Dr. Peter Wagner. The Church has to have a clear and defined plan regarding the ministry of casting out demons (first level), a permanent strategy regarding the occult (second level) and, of course, spiritual warfare on a strategic level (third level). I have attested that sometimes, there is an emphasis on the third level without appropriately taking care of the two prior ones. As you will see in Chapter 11, the Bible demonstrates that the apostle Paul battled on those three levels at the same time, with evident results.

Spiritual warfare prayer, together with the demolition of strongholds through prophetic acts, can truly give cities, territories and even entire nations into the hands of believers who are willing to fight for what legally belongs to Christ. I have seen God work profound changes in my country. I saw Him give us a Christian president as a result of the prayers and fasting of a multitude of Guatemalans. Today, my countrymen are witnesses of the progress and blessings we have. It is known that in Guatemala the number of believers surpasses forty percent of the population. Personally, I believe the blessing of evangelism is due to the open heaven we enjoy as a result of prophetic intercession.

I am a completely convinced witness that intercessory prayer is the way to change history. It is the way to affect our nations, recover lost territory, and give our children the inheritance of a redeemed land for Christ.

I believe with all my heart that spiritual warfare is nothing more than a name, a current trend, a novelty, if you wish, that

God has used in this time to bring us back to His original plan, teaching us what He expects of His Church.

My desire is to present to you through these pages a perspective of spiritual warfare from the point of view of a local pastor. I will show you our conclusions, mistakes, and achievements. From a biblical basis, I will illustrate each point I make with examples of what we have lived. I am convinced that theory is not enough, but also the practical application of the concepts is necessary. I will show that our results, in addition to being tangible, are measurable. Only in this way will we know that we are producing fruit for the kingdom of God. On the other hand, I will present you with what I call an integral vision of spiritual warfare. This includes a three-point study constituting the three parts of the human being: spirit, soul, and body. This will help us formulate a global strategy of spiritual warfare transforming all areas of our society.

Added to the above, I will continually use diagrams and illustrations to better explain the concepts I will share with you. Feel free to use them to teach others. Those who have seen me teach know that I use charts and frequently use synonyms to make myself clear. I perceive this according to the principle spoken by our Lord Jesus Christ in the gospel of Matthew 13:23 (NIV), "But the one who received the seed that fell on good soil is the man who hears the word and understands it. He produces a crop, yielding a hundred, sixty or thirty times what was sown." This is to say that it isn't enough to hear, but it is imperative to understand, if one wants to bear fruit for Him.

I am a pastor, totally convinced of the usefulness of the message of spiritual warfare as a message that has an effect on our lives. It makes us become aware of the spiritual reality surrounding us. Much has been said about the Western world vision—the way in which Western cultures perceive the spiritual world. It is said that this particular mentality hinders us to recognize the effect of the spiritual world on our lives, and the life of the society in which we live. Even if the Latin Americans are a little more open to spiritual realities, it is also true that we have not recognized that the roots of many of our social problems are essentially spiritual. I will try to demonstrate that the message of spiritual warfare includes the responsibility we all have, as members of the body of Christ on earth, in the solution of the problems of our community.

I pray to God that the Holy Spirit comes upon you, and the anointing of the Holy One produces those fruits in your church, city and nation, but above all, in your own life. I pray that while you read the concepts poured out in this book, you will arm yourself with the knowledge and the weapons you need to bring about the victory that Christ has already obtained over the devil. I pray to God that this journey we are taking together will be very productive for you. In concluding, I wish to say I am grateful to you for joining me.

PART ONE

Biblical Basis for Spiritual Warfare

In this section we will study the nature of the conflict called Spiritual Warfare, its origin, its characteristics and, above all, the role the believer plays in this conflict.

Special attention will be given to the description of the kingdoms and their characteristics. In other words, this section will offer us the theoretical basis on which the practice of warfare prayer stands.

1

How I Learned that
Spiritual Warfare Exists

*For since the creation of the world His invisible attributes,
His eternal power and divine nature, have been clearly seen,
being understood through what has been made, so that they
are without excuse.*

ROMANS 1:20

Our local church had at the time about three hundred and
fifty members. Everything seemed to be going fine. We had
recently negotiated some land and we were ready to construct our
first temple. Truly, everything about the buying had been a miracle. The land was located in one of the main avenues of the city,
which made it very valuable. The owner agreed to sell it and gave
us the opportunity of possessing the land even though we had
only paid him the equivalent of one per cent of the value; he also
gave us eight months to make our first payment. Everything
looked promising for us at that moment. We were constructing
the temple and putting forth our best effort to complete the
prescheduled payments. Truly, every month was an absolute miracle. When the eight months were over, with great effort, we made
our first payment, just as had been prescribed. The next goal was

to complete the second payment, eight months from that date, which would give us the right to sign the purchasing contract. However, two or three months later, something we really didn't expect happened. The owner of the land visited me and explained that some people wanted to purchase "our" land from him for a greater amount of money than what we had settled for, in cash. However, he added, "I am a man of my word, and I am not going to break the settlement we already established. But, I ask you to get the rest of the money and pay me as soon as possible." After recovering from the shock, we started to pray and call upon the Lord for His help. He filled us with favor and we acquired a financial loan. Nevertheless, one year later, our problems grew worse. The economic situation in the whole country had changed. Interest rates had risen and we had been left with an unfinished building, with no floor or walls, only roof and columns. And if this wasn't enough, now the bank was asking us for a capital payment that was much higher than had been expected. In this way our unpaid bills began to accumulate.

While our financial needs were growing, we inevitably transmitted that same pressure to the congregation, and, to our dismay, we started watching many families abandon the church. Our membership declined from three hundred fifty to two hundred eighty.

It was a very difficult time and maybe the worst was what was going on inside my heart. We were doing everything we knew, praying, fasting, believing, and confessing, but nothing happened. Many times I found myself crying, trying to find an answer. Why didn't God listen to us? And if He did, why didn't He answer us? I cannot describe with words what I was living. There was something inside me that was dying.

Once and again I prayed (and cried) saying, "God, why don't

You help us? We need that money for your church." But there seemed to be no answer. I was a step away from desperation. Frankly, I needed God to intervene quickly; little did I know how soon He was going to respond.

THE INVISIBLE MANIFESTS

One Saturday morning, taking advantage of the church offices being empty, and wanting to be alone, I knelt down to pray, leaning on a stool of my bureau. I must be sincere. In those days what I did was more crying than praying. I was praying when, suddenly, something amazing happened. It was a vision or something that was happening in the spiritual world, I cannot say with precision. What I can assure you is that what I lived in the following moments was absolutely real for me. I was submerged in prayer when suddenly the stool where I was leaning started to elevate and quickly disappeared. Instead of the stool, there was an enormous white snake coiled there. It looked furious and its eyes looked straight at me; I remember, as if it were yesterday, its fixed, menacing look. Its eyes were red, profound, and charged with hate. It seemed as if it had been asleep and now was filled with wrath because someone had come to bother it. Of course, that someone was myself, and in that moment, I was trembling with fear. I was literally trembling. My first intention was to leave the place immediately and find help. It is true that in my work as a pastor I had participated in deliverances, and seen demonic manifestations, but nothing compared with what I was living in those moments.

Without taking my eyes off the serpent, I quickly calculated how many steps it would take to reach the door. Would I have time to get out? I wanted to run, flee. I was confused and frightened. I turned to the door and was just a few steps from it, when something started to happen inside me. From my chest suddenly came a voice with power and authority. It was the voice of the Lord Jesus Christ, that said, "Isn't My name enough? Is the authority of My name not enough for you?" I soon understood that I wasn't permitted to look for help. But at the same time, I wasn't alone. He was with me.

In that instant, this scripture became real in my heart: "You are from God, little children, and have overcome them; because greater is He who is in you than he who is in the world" (1 John 4:4). Therefore, I went back to where that snake was. It was very large, about ten meters long and about twenty centimeters in diameter.

When I looked into its eyes, I noticed that there was no fear in them, no fear at all. While I trembled, I started to rebuke it in the name of Jesus Christ, to cast it out of that place, while countless questions crossed my mind. Was I imagining what was happening? Was what I was experiencing real? What did it mean? How had that serpent come to that place? The intensity of the battle increased and I noticed how the Word of God that came out of my lips and the name of Jesus started to fill me with faith. In a given instant, I saw its eyes and I noticed that they didn't show the same confidence. I could see that what the serpent was losing in confidence, I was gaining. Unexpectedly I could feel that fear had disappeared from me, and the serpent started to uncoil. The fight was tougher by the moment and I soon saw fear in its eyes. I was obtaining victory. Later I would learn that I was only applying, executing the victory of Jesus Christ upon all principality and power. The serpent backed away and suddenly, traversing the wall, it went into the street. To my great surprise, I did the same and we found ourselves in the middle of Sixth Avenue. I was pursuing it, rebuking it in the name of Jesus Christ. I ordered it, with all authority, to flee. And that is exactly what it did. I went after it for several blocks and it moved with greater speed by the moment, fleeing, afraid.

When I came back to my senses, I stayed in my office for a long time, asking myself what the experience I had just meant. One thing was clear. I had obtained a victory, but over what?

The following day, Sunday, I described what had happened during my preaching, even if I still didn't have an explanation. What followed was extraordinary.

A church member, Mario Roberto, went to visit the family of his sister, Carolina, who had not been to the service that Sunday. When he told them what I had said, Carolina started to cry uncontrollably. Her husband and Mario Roberto, worried, asked her what was happening. She told them, "I just had a vision right now in which I saw Pastor Harold taking out and pursuing that snake through Sixth Avenue until it ends. But when the snake came to join its mother, it didn't seem big anymore. It didn't even seem to be a snake, but a worm. The mother snake, that one was really large."

As if this wasn't enough, that same Sunday, while one of our pastors was having lunch with his in-laws, he commented what had happened to me. His father-in-law became interested and started asking questions; coincidentally, he had worked in that exact place and knew the house where we now had the offices of the church. Oscar's father-in-law described the place exactly and added, "I am not surprised with what happened because just there, where the pastor has his stool, is where large sums of money were kept in a safe box." And he continued describing some tragic events that had taken place there which had money as a common denominator.

Everything started making sense. In one way or another, that serpent was a being that represented a spiritual entity that seemed to be "the guardian" of the money. In a twinkling of an eye, the things that were hurting my faith were dissipated. Verses 12 and 13 of chapter 10 in the book of Daniel seemed to resound inside my mind.

"Then he said to me, 'Do not be afraid, Daniel, for from the first day that you set your heart on understanding this and on humbling yourself before your God, your words were heard, and I have come in response to your words. But the prince of the kingdom of Persia was withstanding me for twenty-one days; then behold, Michael, one of the chief princes, came to help me, for I had been left there with the kings of Persia.'"

In an instant, I received the answer that would later on produce a great effect on my life. The message is very simple, but profound, and I state it like this: God is a God of blessing (3 John 2), who desires your health and prosperity. God is a God that answers the prayers of His children (Matthew 7:7), but these answers, these blessings can find resistance and opposition as described in the case of Daniel. That opposition can and must be conquered through prayer and fasting. In other words, we have a very active role in obtaining our blessings. If we do not receive the answer to our prayers it is not because God doesn't want to give it to us, but because there is an invisible enemy that wants to put obstacles to our receiving, an enemy that *it is possible* to defeat.

This principle was destined to open our understanding and take us to victory. I soon learned to apply it in each area of our lives. God wants the Church to grow. He wants His children to have abundance and blessing. He desires marriages to be happy and nations to have peace and prosperity. When we are not living in this victory we shouldn't assume that God is to blame. We shouldn't let our faith in prayer dismay either, believing that God answers only "sometimes." Even if it seems strange to you, there are many believers who have not developed faith in prayer because they have not understood this principle. God always answers prayer (Matthew 7:7–8; 21:22). If we do not see the manifestation of the answer, the responsibility is not God's. Surely, He already sent the answer but, many times, at the same time that God sends the blessing, the devil sends forces of darkness to prevent us from receiving it. Now, the responsibility rests upon us, to whom God has given authority over all forces of the enemy (Luke 10:19; Ephesians 3:20).

In regards to the weapons to overcome opposition, the Word of God and the name of Jesus make up the instruments of victory.

THE MANIFESTATION OF THE ANSWER OF GOD

The days that followed were of special learning. The economic pressure had been such that we were totally overwhelmed, and after consulting with the Lord, we decided to sell the land in order to be released from debt. Less than two years had passed since we negotiated the land and the conditions of our national economy were not favorable to us. This being the case, we imagined that our best option was to sell the land at the same price we had purchased it for. We would take our steel roof and start again in another place. God had a different and much better plan because the obstacle had already been removed.

By this time, our debt had increased because of the increase in interest rates and because of different pending payments. Contrary to what I believed, not many people showed interest in buying, but there was a company that was interested, so we agreed on a meeting with their representatives for the next Thursday morning.

Wednesday night, during our regular service, something unexpected happened. We were visited by a real estate agent who wished to promote the sale of our property. I rejected his offer from the start because we could not afford to pay a sales commission. However, this man insisted again and again. He insisted so much that he decided to call my house that same night. During the conversation, and in his eagerness to convince me, he said, "I could sell that land for a good price." I answered, "How much is a good price?" His answer greatly impacted me. In his opinion, the land was worth exactly twice the amount we were hoping to receive.

I want to ask you, dear reader, to put yourself in my place for a moment. The news was too good for the state in which we were at that time. So, I finished the conversation with the same negativity as at the beginning, but, later on, I could not stop thinking about that amount. I called a brother and asked him to come with me the next day and I told him what had happened. We decided to meet earlier to pray. When the interested party arrived, the meeting developed normally, until the time came for the long awaited question: "How much do you want for the property, Pastor?" Amazed, I heard how the voice came out of my mouth saying exactly double the amount we originally expected. After an instant of silence, the buyer exclaimed, "I agree totally, Pastor. How do you want us to pay you?" If you thought that I almost fell out of my chair, you are right! That is exactly what happened.

I must confess that, with so many emotions, it took me some days to realize that the events that had taken place were not isolated, but were, in fact, a cause and effect relationship. The ministry finances had surely experienced a deliverance. It seemed that the casting out of that serpent—the "guardian of the money"—and the deliverance of the finances were linked. The demon that had prevented us from receiving our supernatural provision had been conquered in the first of many spiritual battles that were to come.

It is interesting to recognize that in our case, the greatest lessons and the greatest battles have been linked to the land we have purchased as a ministry. So, let us advance in time, and join me in the next land that God gave us.

We were excited due to having obtained an extraordinary miracle. Because of God's direct intervention, we had been able to purchase another property. I must add, for His glory, this second land was twelve times larger than the former one. The size was really extraordinary: Two hundred meters in the front by one hundred fifty meters deep. Actually, it was a mansion surrounded by open land. The house was so large that with some modifications we were able to house El Shaddai Christian School there. Today, the school has five hundred students, and in the open area we can build a large temple and have parking space for hundreds of cars.

Everything related to the purchase and payment was absolutely supernatural. God gave us favor with the owner, so that we could buy the first part and, at the same time, lease the rest. You will understand that we did not want to sink in debt again. I would like to have the space to tell you all that happened, but I think it digresses from the theme we are discussing today.

We consulted with the Lord and designed a plan according to His words. We would use the facilities that were already there and, as a sanctuary, we put up a tent, following the instructions He gave us. We would remain in that tent for the time necessary to pay for the land and afterwards, we would construct a temple. As you can imagine, by this time, I was full of excitement and energy. As far as we knew, the terrible episode of the white serpent was surpassed. Be it what it may, it was buried in the past. That was what we believed, but how far we were from the truth!

THE SERPENT MOTHER APPEARS

I traveled to Oklahoma, in the United States, to purchase the tent, while in Guatemala, preparations were made to install it. The congregation, with the enthusiasm and love of God, was ready to work. One of them lent us a tractor to level the land where we would build a concrete platform, which would serve as the floor for the tent. The tent maker had sent us the instructions with the necessary preparation work. Everyone was excited when quite by accident the tractor driver discovered a problem. Because it was the rainy season in Guatemala, the land was very humid and tractor work became complicated. There was a small hill in the back of our land. It was a hill that, without a doubt, occupied a space that sooner or later we would need. So the tractor, not to lose time while the land dried enough to continue working, went to remove that mound of soil.

When I came back from the trip, I found totally unexpected news. I was informed that the authorities had stopped the construction. In fact, we were prohibited from continuing construction because of a problem that we didn't understand. The authorities of the Institute of Anthropology and History had summoned us, and we went.

When we arrived on Monday morning, we found an uncomfortable, even hostile, environment. When we asked the reason for our summoning, the answer was amazing. "You have been damaging a national monument, a pre-Columbian monument." Practically, we could not believe our ears. I took a moment to comprehend it. I did not have the slightest idea that there could be a pre-Columbian monument in that part of the city. Yes, we all knew of the existence of archeological remains in the other side of the city, but that was more than twenty kilometers away from where we were.

Still surprised with what had been said to us, when we asked what monument it was, the answer came promptly. It is "The Great Mound of the Snake of the Valley of Guatemala."

The Great Mound of the Snake? The reader can imagine the impression that this answer made on us. So that meant that the promontory of soil that crossed the back of our property was a national monument? A snake? A series of thoughts started to swarm my mind. It was like a puzzle that started to take form, and my mind was relating to what we were hearing with the experience of the white snake.

Was there any relationship? Was this really the second part of the revelation, according to Carolina's vision? I was totally prepared to get to the end of this. So that same day we organized a group of persons that would assist me in this journey. Little did we know that what we were actually doing was taking our first steps in spiritual mapping, and that in time, they would become what now is our more experienced and closer group of intercessors.

Our first step was to obtain as much information as possible in libraries and bookstores. Little did we imagine the great effect these events would have in our lives, ministry, and above all, in our country.

We read many books, visited research centers, and interviewed experts. That is how we found there was a specific book dealing with the subject.[1] The interview with the author gave us a greater understanding. Now we knew the Mound of the Snake was handmade about two hundred years before Christ, that it was constructed in the form of an elongated pyramid and that its constructors were the indigenous people that populated these lands for the first time.

Its measures are impressive. It is thirty meters wide, fifteen meters high and even today, with all the growth of the city, it is more than four kilometers long. It is believed that it was originally twenty-two kilometers long, but most astonishing is the fact that such a structure had gone unnoticed by the population of the city.

So that you can get an idea of the subtlety of the enemy and the importance of these things being discovered and rightfully treated spiritually, I will tell you that this mound was totally hidden for centuries. It was only discovered slightly over thirty years ago. It sounds absolutely unbelievable, but that is the truth. It so happens that in the time of the Spaniards, they constructed an aqueduct to transport water, and the constructor found it useful to place the aqueduct over the crest of the snake. Where the pre-Columbian structure presented a rupture, the Royal Water Keeper built colonial arches for the aqueduct. This is why, for many years, it was thought that this promontory was just an artificial covering of land, built to reinforce and protect the arches of the colonial structure, due to the frequent earthquakes that have smitten these regions.[2]

Day after day we gathered more information and each night we prayed to God asking ourselves what all this was and where it would take us. Practically all of our questions had been answered, but there was something that still disquieted me. It was really the most important question. Why had the mound been built? We found nothing more about that subject than the following expression, which geared our research in a totally new direction: It was built for "ceremonial" use. The word ceremonial brought the word idolatry to my mind, and I purposed to know more about that snake that had been given so much dedication and effort in the past. What or who was it?

We would soon find an answer to that doubt. It is difficult for me to give a detailed account of all the authors we read as well as all the people we interviewed during that time. It is enough to say that soon we bumped into the figure worshiped by almost every pre-Columbian culture of Latin America: Quetzalcoatl, the flying serpent.

MEETING THE GOD OF THE PRE-COLUMBIAN CULTURES

We learned that the main American cultures, the Mayas, Aztecs and Incas, held their cult of the feathered serpent or the flying serpent as a common denominator. The one called Quetzalcoatl, Kukulcan, or Gucumatz in Meso America, was called Viracocha in South America.

As one who perceives he is doing something important, we moved swiftly. We went from one conclusion to the next, with the clear sensation of being guided by the Holy Spirit. Some of the clues we found were from the natural realm; others were intellectual and, clearly, once and again, the Word guided us in the way to follow.

To someone who had never questioned the influence of principalities and powers, it was very impressive to see how God uncovered the veil that had hidden them. In spite of studying a god that belonged to an ancient culture, we were clearly conscious that it was something that remained alive and active. It seemed that God was opening our understanding so that our eyes could see the invisible. Even today, it is absolutely providential how God put all that information before us.

While we conducted our investigation about that god worshiped by ancient cultures, we realized that to obtain a complete result we needed an approach that would cover various perspectives. We had to consider the existence of monuments, archeological remains, and the clue places that were a necessity to visit. We totally committed ourselves to those tasks. In addition to reading a great amount of literature, we interviewed authorities in the world of anthropology, archeology, history, and geography. We did not spare any effort, and most of all, we looked to the Lord and His continual guidance. Frankly, I believe I am not able to express with total justice how supernatural this walk was.

The cult to Quetzalcoatl began with the first inhabitants of Meso America, the Chanes, whose name literally means snake men, or children of the serpent. These, as the Mayas that came after them, worshiped the rattlesnake, believing that it was a holy animal due to its ability to measure time. We must remember that the Mayan culture stood out precisely for its studies of mathematics, astronomy, and above all, what concerns chronology. They invented a calendar that is known to be even more exact than the calendar we use today. The rattlesnake has the particularity of adding a rattle each year of its life, in such a way that when you count its rattles, you can know the age of the crotalus. Further-more, this reptile changes its fangs exactly every twenty days, from which they took the basis of twenty days for each month of their calendar.

It is important here to notice that the Aztec calendar is also a crotalic-like solar stone. That means that the complete calendar is a representation of what for them was worthy of worship: the sun and the serpent. We should not forget that serpent worship is always solar worship.

Each year, during the spring solstice, this serpent undergoes a particular process. Its skin becomes opaque and dry, all its body acquires a gray-like color, a veil falls over its eyes, as would a cataract, and abruptly the viper breaks its covering, abandons it and emerges with a new skin, alive and fresh. Then, it adds a new rattle. This phenomenon is called *caput zijil,* which means, "to be born again." If we add to this that the number four is the number of the sun and of Quetzalcoatl—of whom is said that he died for his people and came back to life on the fourth day—we will see that we are facing a falsification of Christ.

This serpent inspired all art in the Mayan, Aztec, Toltec, and Inca cultures. We could well call them serpentine cultures, when we observe that, from the architecture of their pyramids to the design of their dresses (*huipiles*), all come from the design of serpent skin.

For the Mayas, the cult of the serpent took on such importance that they went to the extreme of taking two tablets to pressure the skull of their children and, in the process, deform them. They would file down their children's teeth and voluntarily make them cross-eyed, in an effort to make them physically similar to the serpent. All of this only confirms the Word of God that says:

"But their idols are silver and gold, made by the hands of men. They have mouths, but cannot speak; eyes, but they cannot see; they have ears, but cannot hear; noses, but they cannot smell; they have hands, but cannot feel, feet, but they cannot walk; nor can they utter a sound with their throats. *Those who make them will be like them,* and so will all who trust in them" (Psalm 115:4–8, NIV).

It came to my attention that a researcher called José Díaz Bolio, from Mérida, Yucatán, Mexico, discovered the crotalic cult in the Mayan culture in 1942, and in spite of multiple evidences presented by him, no one paid attention to his studies. I had the opportunity of reading almost all his numerous books and of visiting him in his home. One night he told me how they had expelled him from the archeological society because they did not believe his affirmations about the serpent being the basis of the culture. The next morning we visited Chichén Itzá for the first time, where I observed dozens of buildings forming the site. Of them, maybe seventy-five have been restored, and on one of them alone I personally counted more than two hundred crotalic symbols. How is it possible that a fact of this magnitude could go unnoticed by the majority, as with the Great Mound of the Snake of the Valley of Guatemala?[3]

We are living in special times when we can see that God has decided that His Church is ready to receive from Him "the treasures of darkness, riches stored in secret places, so that [we] may know that [He is] the Lord, the God of Israel, who summons [us] by name" (Isaiah 45:3, NIV). Surely God is not only going to give us the hidden treasures and secrets, but He will also "go before [us] and level the mountains; [He] will break down gates of bronze and cut through bars of iron," (Isaiah 45:2, NIV) because "the battle is the Lord's, and He will give all of [them] into our hands" (1 Samuel 17:47, NIV).

THE CRUCIAL MOMENT

Without a doubt, the most important moment for us came when we found this principality in the Bible. We could barely believe our eyes. Through the book of Isaiah, God was confirming our findings.

"Do not rejoice, all you of Philistia, because the rod that struck you is broken; for out of the serpent's root will come forth a viper, and its offspring will be a fiery *flying serpent*" (Isaiah 14:29, NKJV).

"The burden against the beasts of the South. Through a land

of trouble and anguish, from which come the lioness and lion, the viper and fiery *flying serpent*, they will carry their riches on the backs of young donkeys and their treasures on the humps of camels, to a people who shall not benefit them" (Isaiah 30:6, NKJV).

We had only started to understand the importance of what we had before us. We realized that our country—actually the countries of what is called Meso America—had been handed over to, dedicated to, or given over to this evil spirit. From there branch many of the characteristics of the cult that are still operative today in our countries.

Now I understood what had really happened to these cultures of pre-Hispanic America. God, in His mercy, had given every man an opportunity. He had given His testimony, but they rejected Him and in their self-deceit, they became corrupted, leaving an inheritance of curse, darkness, and pain to the next generations.

"In the past He let all nations go their own way. *Yet He has not left Himself without testimony:* He has shown kindness by giving you rain from heaven and crops in their seasons; He provides you with plenty of food and fills your hearts with joy" (Acts 14:16–17, NIV).

"Since what may be known about God is plain to them, because God has made it plain to them. For since the creation of the world God's invisible qualities—His eternal power and divine nature—have been clearly seen being understood from what has been made, so that men are without excuse. *For although they knew God, they neither glorified Him as God nor gave thanks to Him, but their thinking became futile and their foolish hearts were darkened. Although they claimed to be wise, they became fools and exchanged the glory of the immortal God for images made to look like mortal man and birds and animals and reptiles. Therefore God gave them over to the sinful desires of their hearts* to sexual impurity for the degrading of their bodies with one another. They exchanged the truth of God for a lie, and worshiped and served created things rather than the Creator—who is forever praised. Amen" (Romans 1:19–25, NIV).

Certainly, the Mayas went through all that degenerative process which is provoked by idolatry. From the adoration of God, they placed their eyes upon man, and with this sin they became corrupted, going, as says in James 3:15, from the wisdom that comes from heaven to a wisdom that is "earthly, unspiritual, of the devil." From there, they lowered themselves to worshiping birds (the quetzal), animals (the jaguar), and ended up worshiping reptiles (the rattlesnake).

During all of the research process, our attention was powerfully drawn to the bloodthirstiness of that cult—the human sacrifices—and the unique way in which the sacrifices were conducted.

We learned that what was called the Mayan ball game was actually an allegoric ceremony—an astronomical ritual[4]—that involved two teams of seven persons. All of them belonged to the community; there were no foreigners, prisoners or slaves among them. On the contrary, the best of the youth in the community were chosen. The most important moment came after the game, when the captain of the winning team proceeded to sacrifice the captain of the opposing team. While the loser was held on a platform specially built for that purpose, the victor dug a special utensil (many of which can be found in museums) into his chest and extracted the still beating heart of the victim to offer it to Quetzalcoatl. This was how they performed the dedication, through a blood covenant, of which we will speak in detail in the book *Kings and Priests*.

The natural knowledge we were obtaining served as basis for

the revelation of the Holy Spirit. *What we understood is that, even today in our nations, some of these behavioral patterns are operative.* While it is true that the ball game does not exist any more, and there are no more human sacrifices in that same fashion, the bloodshed through death caused by one brother against the other continues. Many of the Latin American countries (and others of course) have experienced revolutionary or guerrilla movements, and in each of these cases, the process is the same. They are fratricidal wars with Guatemalans murdering Guatemalans, Nicaraguans against Nicaraguans, etc. Brothers shed their brother's blood, thus defiling the land (Numbers 35:33). We understood that the intervention of the church is necessary to settle those ancestral problems spiritually if we want to see the freedom of our nations.[5]

When I did the above research, Mexico was an exception to my hypothesis. However, some time after, the Zapatist Army of National Liberation emerged as one more movement of the ones that have brought so much pain to our people.

Little by little we discovered how deep the roots of the serpent cult were in our culture. Even the City of Guatemala had been designed in a spiral, as the rattlesnake lies when it is secure and is not afraid of an attack (see Luke 11:21).

Clearly, in Guatemala, the Quetzal is not only the national bird, but also the name of our currency. I found it very revealing that when examining the ornamental patterns of our bills, the number of crotalic or serpentine symbols in them increased in direct proportion to the devaluation of the currency. Before this devaluation, our bills had pictures of nature, or civic feats, like the signing of our independence. All of a sudden, as if there had been a mastermind behind it, the designs and pictures in the bills started to change. For example, they ranged from having images of the jaw of the Palenque serpent to the extreme of having twenty-one crotalic symbols in the fifty quetzal bill.

Somehow, I was starting to understand the existence of a very important spiritual principle. *The natural, what we can see, what is perceived by our senses, is only a reflection of the spiritual, of the invisible.*

The apostle Paul stated it like this:

"While we look not at the things which are seen, but at the things which are not seen; for the things which are seen are temporal, but the things which are not seen are eternal" (2 Corinthians 4:18).

Through all of this information, God was speaking to us, letting us know that the situation of our nation was due to spiritual circumstances—to the direct action of forces that were hidden to the human eye—but that are absolutely real.

IT IS TIME TO DO SOMETHING

The puzzle pieces were rapidly coming into place. Our country was at a crossroads and we had the key. The Bible had spoken to us again and again of a battle.

"For we do not wrestle against flesh and blood, but against principalities, against powers, against the rulers of the darkness of this age, against spiritual hosts of wickedness in the heavenly places" (Ephesians 6:12, NKJV).

"For though we walk in the flesh, we do not war according to the flesh. For the weapons of our warfare are not carnal but mighty in God for pulling down strongholds, casting down arguments, and every high thing that exalts itself against the knowledge of God, bringing every thought into captivity to the obedience of Christ" (2 Corinthians 10:3–5, NKJV).

We were suddenly invaded by a sense of urgency. God was putting before us a revelation, giving us a great responsibility. We assumed He expected an answer from us, a reaction. A brother, precious intercessor, gave us a very clear and concise message from the Lord. It was the word found in Esther 4:14: "For if you remain silent at this time, relief and deliverance will arise for the Jews from another place and you and your father's house will perish. And who knows whether you have not attained royalty for such a time as this?"

I clearly remember the place where God spoke to me one morning, during a pastor meeting. There, I conceived the vision. There, the project called "Jesus is Lord of Guatemala" was born, with the vision of recruiting a great army of intercessors to bring about the redemption of our country from the hands of the enemy by breaking all covenants placed over our country that were not from the Lord.

We decided to use a very special textbook about prayer. We printed seventy thousand copies of *Prayer, the Key to Revival* by Dr. David Yonggi Cho. We started interceding for Guatemala and we had very exciting times, some of which will be written as testimonies or illustrations in the next pages of this book. Without a doubt, the Lord was with us all that time and He certainly, "with severe sword, great and strong, will punish Leviathan the fleeing serpent, Leviathan that twisted serpent, and He will slay the reptile that is in the sea" (Isaiah 27:1, NKJV).

It was an intense moment in which we lived extraordinary experiences. Our church fully participated in the vision and became a praying church, a warring church. We saw our congregation grow, multiplying by seven in only two years. A member of the church was a candidate to the presidency of the country, and through prayer, we saw him go from a three percent popularity to the triumph in the general elections obtaining, in only ninety days, the largest percentage of votes in the history of the country.

In those days we made many discoveries in the area of spiritual mapping, prophetic acts, decrees, and many other things we will discuss at the appropriate time.

We lived an impressive time of miracles. The road to a new Guatemala was on its way.

One of the most important lessons we learned is that spiritual warfare is not a sporadic act. It is not something done today and abandoned tomorrow. No.

If we study the Bible we will see that we live in a constant situation of spiritual warfare. This is a truth that once known is never abandoned. To get involved in spiritual warfare just for a season, and then retire, is like standing on an anthill, killing some ants, and then remaining standing there. You know the rest of the story.

Spiritual warfare really constitutes the normal way of life for the believers that have been redeemed by Christ from the slavery of the devil. Once on this side, we are no longer his slaves. We now belong to the kingdom of light and our natural enemy constitutes darkness. While we remain on the earth we will have an enemy that is in continual war against us. We had better learn what the battle is all about.

2

Description of the Conflict

I will go before you and make the rough places smooth; I will shatter the doors of bronze, and cut through their iron bars. And I will give you the treasures of darkness, and hidden wealth of secret places, in order that you may know that it is I, the Lord, the God of Israel, who calls you by your name.

ISAIAH 45:2,3

If we wish to define spiritual warfare, we should start by establishing that there are two kingdoms at war in existence, opposing one another, in open confrontation. One kingdom belongs to God and the other to the devil. Not in vain is he called "the ruler of this world" or "the prince of the power of the air" (John 16:11 and Ephesians 2:2). Spiritual warfare is the conflict between these two kingdoms, the kingdom of light and the kingdom of darkness, which contend for the eternal destiny of mankind.

THE DIFFERENCE BETWEEN EVERLASTING AND ETERNAL LIFE

There are two kinds of life. One, which all human beings share, is everlasting life. The other, an exclusive characteristic of believers, is eternal life. Everlasting life comes from the fact that the human spirit and soul never die, that is, they will live forever. Eternal life is the nature of God, the *zoe* life that God gives man when he is born again. The difference between them is that he who has received eternal life will spend eternity with God, while the one that does not receive the Lord Jesus Christ as Lord and Savior, will spend eternity without Him (Matthew 25:46; John 3:36 and John 5:24).

The conflict we call spiritual warfare specifically deals with this issue. The kingdoms contend for the eternal destiny of men. The kingdom of heaven presents battle, as a manifestation of the purpose of God, "who desires all men to be saved and to come to the knowledge of the truth" (1 Timothy 2:4), while the kingdom of darkness wants to keep all men in bondage, separated from God, until their eternal perdition.

Second Corinthians 4:4 says: "The god of this age has blinded the minds of the unbelievers, so that they cannot see the light of the gospel of the glory of Christ, who is the image of God." That is the reason why the word *evangelism* becomes so important in the study of this issue. Evangelism makes the entire difference between a humanity that reigns eternally with Christ or one that is reduced to eternal chastisement. Sometimes I am under the impression that, in general, the body of Christ has not understood what is at stake.

CHARACTERS INVOLVED IN THE CONFLICT
(Figure 1.1)

The concept of a kingdom speaks to us of a king, subjects, territory, a given language and, of course, a set of laws that rule that kingdom. Clearly, each of the kingdoms has an army and these are the ones who fight the battle.[6]

DESCRIPTION OF THE CONFLICT

Characters Involved in the Conflict

KINGDOM OF LIGHT	KINGDOM OF DARKNESS

A. GOD
  • Father
  • Son
  • Holy Spirit
 	
B. ANGELS
 	
C. CHURCH
	A. The devil
	
	B. His hierarchy
	  ❑ principalities
	  ❑ powers
	  ❑ rulers of the darkness of this age
	  ❑ spiritual host of wickedness in heavenly places
	     (EPHESIANS 6:12)
	  ❑ thrones
	     (COLOSSIANS 1:16)
	  ❑ dominions
	  ❑ might
	  ❑ every name that is named, not only in this age, but also in that which is to come
	     (EPHESIANS 1:21)

	Men 2 CORINTHIANS 4:4

(Figure 1.1)

In the kingdom of light we find God in the first place. I call it the Godhead because it includes the Father, the Son, and the Holy Spirit. Next, there is a category of spiritual beings that we call angels. I am totally aware of the existence of archangels, seraphim, cherubim, etc., but I have decided to include them under a single name. And then we have the Church of Jesus Christ, consisting of all men and women who have been saved by the grace and mercy of God.

In the kingdom of darkness we find the devil and his satanic hierarchy conformed by principalities, powers, rulers of the darkness of this age, spiritual hosts of wickedness in the heavenly places, thrones, dominions, principalities, powers, might, and every name that is named, not only in this age but also in that which is to come (Ephesians 6:12; Colossians 1:16 and Ephesians 1:21). I tried to list each of the words that the New King James Version gives us to refer to the forces of evil, avoiding repetitions without getting into the existing argument of who has the greater or lesser rank.

After having placed the active characters of each kingdom in order of battle, we will concentrate on the objective of the conflict: man.

One would feel tempted to place man in the center of the diagram, in the middle of the two kingdoms. However, this would not be correct. Humanity is not in a neutral place, simply because such a place does not exist. Humanity (unredeemed) is on the side of the kingdom of darkness, and the Church (the congregation of the redeemed) is on the side of the kingdom of light. Man always begins his walk on the side of the kingdom of darkness, "for all have sinned and fall short of the glory of God" (Romans 3:23).

Because man begins his walk in the darkness, it is necessary to remove the blinding veil (2 Corinthians 4:3, 4) in order to receive the light of the gospel. This is exactly what can be achieved through intercessory prayer, because intercession, by definition, consists of prayer in favor of another person. If we destroy that veil of blindness through intercession, surely the person for whom we are praying will see before him the glorious light of the gospel of Jesus Christ.

Let me reinforce, here, a concept of vital importance. Many times I hear expressions such as, "They don't want to receive Jesus in this place." That is an absolutely erroneous statement. People who do not receive Jesus do not do it because they do not want to but because they cannot. They have a veil of blindness that prevents the light of the gospel from shining on them. None of us would be able to see the light if we had a veil covering our eyes. It would be necessary to remove the veil in order to see the light of day. That is the reality of nations and cities where the gospel does not find easy entrance. There is a veil that needs to be removed. If you are asking yourself about the possibility of removing that blindness, the answer is a firm "Yes." "For though we walk in the flesh, we do not war according to the flesh, for the weapons of our warfare are not of the flesh, but divinely powerful for the destruction of fortresses [strongholds, NIV]. We are destroying speculations and every lofty thing raised up against the knowledge of God, and we are taking every thought captive to the obedience of Christ" (2 Corinthians 10:3–5).

If man begins his walk in the kingdom of darkness,[7] how can he come to the kingdom of light? Colossians 1:13–14 says that it is God who rescues us from the dominion of darkness and brings us into the kingdom of the Son He loves, in whom we have redemption [by his blood], the forgiveness of sins. This means that literally, God extracts us from under the dominion of darkness and, delivering us from there, transfers us to the other kingdom, the kingdom of His beloved Son. It is through the sacrifice of Christ that we obtain the way out of darkness into the light. Where before there was fathomless abyss, now there is a Way, Christ.

This is when the conflict begins. Let me explain why. We were all enslaved to Satan; we were dead in trespasses and sins in which we once walked according to the course of this world, according to the prince of the power of the air, the spirit who now works in the sons of disobedience *among whom also we all once conducted ourselves* (see Ephesians 2:1–3, NKJV). We served the devil, we followed him and lived with a darkened understanding, as expressed in Ephesians 4:18. But one day, God, in His mercy, freed us from the power of darkness and transferred us into the kingdom of His beloved Son. At that moment we were literally transferred from one kingdom to another. All at once, the ones who were slaves were made free.

The physical position of a believer has been drastically modified. From being under the devil, he has come to be precisely above him (Ephesians 1:22). Automatically, we proceed from dominated to dominators. From being humanity we become the Church. We came out of a kingdom and were received into another one *(Figure 1.2).*

And in that other kingdom, the one of light, we have been given a place, a relationship. Now we are sons of God; we are the head and not the tail; we are above and not under; and the devil that once dominated us is now under the soles of our feet.

The objective of spiritual warfare seeks to rescue or redeem the human race, taking it out from under the power of darkness. This is what we call evangelism. This is the Great Commission God has entrusted to each of His children, "to open their eyes so that they may turn from darkness to light and from the dominion

DESCRIPTION OF THE CONFLICT

Characters Involved in the Conflict

KINGDOM OF LIGHT	KINGDOM OF DARKNESS

D. GOD
  • Father
  • Son
  • Holy Spirit
 	
E. ANGELS
 	
F. CHURCH
 	
HOW?
  EPHESIANS 3:10
  PSALMS 103:20–21
  JEREMIAH 1:9–10; 4:3;
    4:12, and 4:19
	C. The devil
	
	D. His hierarchy
	  ❑ principalities
	  ❑ powers
	  ❑ rulers of the
	    darkness of this age
	  ❑ spiritual host of
	    wickedness in
	    heavenly places
	      (EPHESIANS 6:12)
	  ❑ thrones
	      (COLOSSIANS 1:16)
	  ❑ dominions
	  ❑ might
	  ❑ every name that is
	    named, not only in
	    this age, but also
	    in that which is to
	    come
	      (EPHESIANS 1:21)

The Church COLOSSIANS 1:13	**Men** 2 CORINTHIANS 4:4

(Figure 1.2)

of Satan to God, in order that they may receive forgiveness of sins and an inheritance among those who have been sanctified by faith in Me" (Acts 26:18).

THE RESPONSIBILITY OF THE CHURCH

The process explained earlier takes place when the church undertakes its part in the responsibility, and acts according to the Word of God.

In this sense, Ephesians 3:10–11, NKJV, very clearly describes the function of the church: "to the intent that now the manifold wisdom of God might be made known by the church to the principalities and powers in the heavenly places, according to the eternal purpose which He accomplished in Christ Jesus our Lord."

This Scripture contains very clear instructions. The church is responsible for making the manifold wisdom of God—His Word—known to principalities and powers in the heavenly places. Before, we used to think that winning souls was an exclusive task of the evangelist, and, suddenly, we find that God has given all of us that responsibility. We can work together with him in that commission from the place we are. How good it is to know that a homemaker, an office worker, a child or an elderly person can collaborate in fulfilling God's desire, "who desires all men to be saved and to come to the knowledge of the truth" (1 Timothy 2:4).

This confirms to us that we are part of God's plan, without taking into account if we are or are not full-time ministers. God can and wants to use us. Our prayers will make the eternal difference for a humanity that suffers.

Ephesians 3:10 explains that the church is the one called to pronounce the Word of God. According to the American Heritage Dictionary, one of the meanings of the word *pronounce* is "to state officially and formally; declare," placing us in the position of proclaiming what God has already decreed.

The Scripture adds precisely whom the church is to talk to, and where this action is to take place: "to the principalities and powers in the heavenly places."[8]

Here, a fundamental question is posed. If the principalities and powers are found in the high places, according to Ephesians 6:12, why does the Bible ask us to make known the manifold wisdom of God to the principalities and powers in the heavenly places? The difference between the high places (Ephesians 6:12, KJV[21]) and heavenly places (Ephesians 3:10, KJV[21]) will shed much light on our study.

The heavenly places are superior, much higher than the high places. It is a biblical fact that there are three heavens (1 Corinthians 12:2). While principalities and powers of the evil one operate in high places, the hosts of God[9] inhabit the heavenly places as is demonstrated in Revelation 5.

Something impressive happens when the church makes the manifold wisdom of God known in the heavenly places. That word leaves the mouth of the believer and reaches those heavenly places, first going through the high places. Let me illustrate this principle with an example. When a believer practices warfare prayer and, fulfilling the Ephesians 5:11 principle, rebukes the forces of darkness, this is what happens even if we cannot see it with our natural eyes: When the Word of God is expressed, it goes out like a torrent of light. That is why the Bible says, "The unfolding of Thy words gives light; it gives understanding to the simple" (Psalms 119:130). The light of the spoken Word advances without stopping; it reaches the high places, and it continues on until it reaches the heavenly places. While passing the high places, the Word reaches the principalities and powers, the rulers of darkness of this world, and the spiritual wickedness in high places, and it covers them with light. Remember that "The light shines in the darkness, and the darkness has not overcome it" (John 1:5, RSV). But the effect does not finish there. The light of the Word continues advancing until it reaches the heavenly places, where it finds the angels of light, and it mobilizes them to apply and effect the official statement dictated by God through His Word.

Psalms 103:20–21, NKJV, says, "Bless the LORD, you His angels, who excel in strength, who do His word, heeding the voice of His word. Bless the LORD, all you His hosts, you ministers of His, who do His pleasure."

It is important to understand the type of participation God expects from His church in spiritual warfare. What a great responsibility we have! In God's creation, the human being is the only one who possesses the ability to speak and the mandate to do it, pronouncing the Scripture to principalities and powers. Today there are billions of people in the world who have never heard about Jesus. What a difference from the first church that filled the known lands with the gospel. Painfully we have to admit that the church has not fulfilled the fundamental mandate of the Lord. We have neglected prayer, intercession for the lost, and making the manifold wisdom of God known to the principalities and powers in the heavenly places.

The Lord gave me an excellent example that I have employed many times to illustrate this concept. The legislators of a nation decide to make a law. In this law they establish that a highway speed limit is to be one hundred kilometers per hour. That law would have no practical value unless there was a police force to enforce it. If a person is driving 125 kilometers per hour, breaking the law, in our hypothetical example, the policeman stops him and takes him to court. The judge has a copy of the law in his hands, which establishes the crime, and its corresponding penalty. The jury listens to the case while the accuser and the defender carry out their work. When the trial reaches the end, the accused is declared guilty. The judge dictates the sentence; for example, one hundred days of jail. Now you need the policeman again, as an additional arm of the law, to escort the transgressor to jail. This is called executing, applying the law.

What I want to convey to you is that it is not enough to have the law—you need an executive arm to enforce it. It is the same in the spiritual kingdom. The angels are the ones who carry out the sentence decreed by God in His Word. "Bless the LORD, you His angels, who excel in *strength, who do His word, heeding the voice of His word*" (Ps. 103:20–21, NKJV).

As we saw before, there are three subjects or main characters in the kingdom of light: God, the angels, and the Church. Now, we can determine the work of each one. God has dictated sentence over the forces of evil, as we find in His Word. The Lord Jesus Christ fulfilled the will of the Father, "having canceled the written code, with its regulations, that was against us and that stood opposed to us; He took it, nailing it to the cross. *And having disarmed the powers and authorities, He made a public spectacle of them, triumphing over them by the cross*" (Colossians 2:14–15, NIV). On His part, the Holy Spirit works today through the Church. The direct responsibility of acting is ours. It is we who are in charge of making the manifold wisdom of God known to principalities and powers. When we do it, the angels will obey the Lord's command, doing His word, in the invisible kingdom. In our example, God would be the legislator; the Church would be the judge, and the angels the police force.

As you can see, the angels obey the "voice" of His Word. Logically, one does not expect action from them if the church does not fulfill its part of "pronouncing" the Word. However, if the church diligently fulfills its part, the angels will accomplish theirs, because they are "ministering spirits sent to serve those who will inherit salvation" (Hebrews 1:14). The evangelization and transformation of the nations depend, then, on the faithfulness of the Church.

JEREMIAH 1:10—AN IMPORTANT REVELATION

"See, I have appointed you this day over the nations and over the kingdoms, to pluck up and to break down, to destroy and to overthrow, to build and to plant" (Jeremiah 1:10).

My prayer life and the way I perceived spiritual reality drastically changed when God revealed this scripture to my heart. In it, there are four verbs of destruction, and two of construction. When I studied these four actions in detail—uproot, tear down, destroy, and overthrow—I noticed that after them, absolutely nothing is left. It is then that building and planting follow. I believe we have been very ignorant of the spiritual reality contained in these steps.

Normally, we do something like this: We go somewhere, lease facilities in a corner, and open a church. Then, we wish that people would come on Sunday. We truly believe that is the way things should be done, and in that way we enter enemy territory, without even realizing that there are invisible, spiritual forces there. We spend all our life preaching. Nevertheless, many times—without wanting to be negative—no noticeable effect is produced. Almost half of the world's population has not yet heard the gospel of Jesus Christ. And one of the reasons for this is the mistake we have committed by thinking it is enough to have the best seed, ignoring the condition of the land where it will be planted.

If someone were to give us a piece of land, the best land, the most fertile, and say, "Here, I want to give you this gift. This piece of land has the best soil in this country. It is yours. I have not cultivated it in the last few years, but now, it's for you." Because the land is fertile, it is surely full of thistles, weeds, and shrubs. Would you take the best seeds, maybe the best strawberry seeds of California, and plant them immediately in that piece of land?

Anyone knows that should never be done. First, we need to prepare the land, to uproot and tear down, to destroy, and overthrow. And only when the land is clean is it ready to be built upon and planted. We need to understand this principle that we had not understood until now, in spite of the Word that says, "This is what the LORD says to the men of Judah and Jerusalem: "Break up your unploughed ground and do not sow among thorns" (Jeremiah 4:3, NIV).

What a difference it would make if we first carried out spiritual mapping, then inspected the land, confronted the enemy, and picked up the spoils! (Luke 11:21–23)

THE LANGUAGE OF THE KINGDOMS

As the different nations have their language, spiritual kingdoms also have their own language. In the kingdom of light, the language is called *intercession*. In the kingdom of darkness, the language is *accusation*. As a matter of fact, our Lord, Jesus Christ, is interceding for us precisely at this moment (Romans 8:38 and Hebrews 7:25), while the Bible calls the devil "the accuser of our brothers" (Revelation 12:10). Sadly, many times the members of the body of Christ still use the language they learned in the world—the language of darkness—and walk in the road of accusation. Each time a believer dedicates himself to accuse the brethren and to plant division, he is exercising, in accordance with the devil, the language of the kingdom of darkness.

It saddens me to recognize that many people who have been saved, have yet to learn the language of the kingdom of light, which is none other than intercession. How many people live in absolute ignorance of their task as intercessors, as kings and priests of God Almighty? The Bible calls us fellow laborers with God. There is no higher task than to be the spokesmen of the Almighty. Jeremiah 15:19 says, "Therefore this is what the LORD says: 'If you repent, I will restore you that you may serve Me; if you utter worthy, not worthless words, you will be My spokesman. Let these people turn to you, but you must not turn to them.'" God is expecting that each one of us learn to speak only "whatever is true, whatever is noble, whatever is right, whatever is pure, whatever is lovely, whatever is admirable—if anything is excellent or praiseworthy . . ." (Philippians 4:8, NIV). God expects us to remove from our vocabulary all that is vile. If we do so, we will be as His "mouth."

3

The Origin of
Spiritual Warfare

*The secret things belong to the Lord our God, but those
things which are revealed belong to us and to our children
forever, that we may do all the words of this law.*

DEUTERONOMY 29:29, NKJV

I have found there is the generalized idea that spiritual warfare is
due to what they call the eternal conflict between good and evil.
Nothing is farther from the truth. In this chapter I want to
demonstrate that spiritual warfare is a process that had a beginning and will have an ending. Being aware of this reality will help
us to better understand our function in this conflict.

In addition to understanding when this conflict began, it is
necessary to know the reason of its origin and also how and when
it will end.

The concept of spiritual warfare is linked to the concept of
time. We move daily within the concepts of space and time. It is
very natural in our daily conversation to use expressions like,
"Yesterday I did; tomorrow I will do. I will go here; I will go back
there." It would be difficult for us to ignore temporality in our
speech. However, for God, time is not an important concept. He

is *El Olam,* the eternal God. God's creation is noted because of its eternity. Even if we conceive a future eternity, few know that there was also a past eternity. As a matter of fact, from the study of the Bible we come to the conclusion that the time the Bible describes with detail, and divides in Old and New Testament, is but a parenthesis between eternity past and eternity future.[10]

Searching for the origin of evil, I started in the book of Genesis, one of my favorites, and found myself meditating about the great difference between the first two verses of the Bible. There was something that did not quite fit. It was not easy for me to assimilate the fact that God had created the heavens and the earth and that next, these appeared without form and void. My spirit seemed to perceive a door of information for me to look into.

It did not take long to discover an avalanche of information about this.[11] The biblical evidence about a great abyss of time between verse one and verse two of the book of Genesis, was immense, as immense as is the evidence about the existence of a pre-Adamic world that suffered the effects of a God-decreed judgment. Moses, Isaiah, Ezekiel, Jeremiah, Jesus, Peter, Paul, and John teach extensively on the subject.

Our study begins with the first two verses of the Bible and the abyss that exists between them. Genesis 1:1 states, "In the beginning God created the heavens and the earth." Verse two adds, "And the earth was formless and void, and darkness was over the surface of the deep; and the Spirit of God was moving over the surface of the waters." God is a God of order. It makes no sense that He created the earth and, immediately after, it was found to be without form and void, covered by darkness. It seems to us that between the two verses, there was an occurrence that altered the original order, and left the earth "formless and void."

The prophet Isaiah adds, "For thus says the Lord, who created the heavens, (He is the God who formed the earth and made it. He established it and did not create it a waste place. But formed it to be inhabited), I am the Lord, and there is none else." (Isaiah 45:18, NAS).

In Spanish, the Bible says "I created it, and fixed it." God speaks of two stages. One in which He "created" the earth and one in which He "fixed" it, meaning there was a moment in which the plan of God suffered a variation. God Himself to fulfill His purposes interrupted it. God's action caused a catastrophe, a cataclysm of such magnitude that it motivated God to "fix" it. This is called the judgment over the pre-Adamic creation. Of course, this makes us confront the fact that there was a creation prior to Adam's. I hope not to confuse you. I understand this is a great quantity of information and for some, even new. Continue with me, and we will discover the origin of spiritual warfare together.

At this moment, we will study the first stage together, the one referred to in Genesis, verse one: "In the beginning God created the heavens and the earth." The Word of God teaches us that before our days there was a stage of indefinite length, eternal, characterized by the nonexistence of evil.

To study "eternity past" let us look at the book of the prophet Ezekiel:

"Son of man, take up a lamentation for the king of Tyre, and say to him, 'Thus says the Lord God: "You were the seal of perfection, full of wisdom and perfect in beauty. You were in Eden, the garden of God; every precious stone was your covering: the sardius, topaz, and diamond, beryl, onyx, and jasper, sapphire, turquoise; and emerald with gold. The workmanship of your timbrels and pipes [of your tambourines and of your flutes— Greens Literal Translation, 1993]—was prepared for you on the day you were created. You were the anointed cherub who covers;

I established you; you were on the holy mountain of God; you walked back and forth in the midst of fiery stones. You were perfect in your ways from the day you were created, till iniquity was found in you. By the abundance of your trading you became filled with violence within, and you sinned; therefore I cast you as a profane thing out of the mountain of God; and I destroyed you, O covering cherub from the midst of the fiery stones. Your heart was lifted up because of your beauty; you corrupted your wisdom for the sake of your splendor; I cast you to the ground, I laid you before kings, that they might gaze at you. You defiled your sanctuaries by the multitude of your iniquities, by the iniquity of your trading; therefore I brought fire from your midst; it devoured you, and I turned you to ashes upon the earth in the sight of all who saw you. All who knew you among the peoples are astonished at you; you have become a horror, and shall be no more forever" (Ezekiel 28:12–19, NKJV).

The Bible speaks to the king of Tyre in this passage, and yet, historically, it is a fact that Tyre never had a king but a prince, as it is well said in verse two of the same chapter. It is a generally accepted concept that this passage is directed to a being, created by God, who in the book of Isaiah receives the name of Lucifer, morning star, son of the dawn; the cherub who would eventually become the devil.

From that moment on, two lines of thought intertwine in our study: the first, in relation to the characteristics of this eternity past, and the second, that refers to this being called Satan.

From the great abundance of information provided us by that Scripture, we come to the following conclusions:

- The cherub created by God was in itself the seal of perfection, full of wisdom and perfect in beauty. The words *seal* and *perfection* speak of the maximum of creation. (See Jude 1:9.)

- He was in Eden, the garden of God.

- His clothing was very particular, "of every precious stone."

- The workmanship of his "tambourines and his flutes" was prepared for him on the day he was created. This is especially important because it says that a) he possessed in himself tambourines and flutes, that is, musical capability and ability; and b) the Bible clearly establishes that this is a created being. This means that it is not an eternal being. There was a day, a moment in time, in which he was created.

- God set this covering cherub in the holy mountain of God. He walked up and down in the midst of the stones of fire. Here we start noticing that the Eden spoken of here is not exactly the Eden we are accustomed to refer to. This Eden is in the holy mountain of God, not in the region where we usually locate the Tigris and Euphrates rivers. While the Eden of Adam gives us an image of an organic kingdom, this garden referred to in the book of Ezekiel speaks of a world of mineral nature. We do not find Adam walking in the midst of the " fiery stones." We do not find him surrounded by precious stones either but by plants, trees, and animals.

- From the day of his creation he was "perfect in all his ways," but there came a day in which everything changed, the day that iniquity was found in him.

- He was filled with iniquity and sinned because of the abundance of his trading, a subject we will discuss later in detail.

- As a consequence, he was cast out of the mountain of God and God destroyed him from the "midst of the fiery stones."

- His heart was lifted up because of his beauty and he corrupted his wisdom for the sake of his splendor.

- The Lord cast him to the ground before kings.

- By the *multitude of his iniquities* and by the *iniquity of his trading,* he defiled his *sanctuaries.* The word sanctuaries together with the tambourines and flutes surely speak to us of worship; therefore, a priesthood.

- God brought forth a fire from his midst that devoured him, and God turned him to ashes upon the earth in the sight of all who saw him.

The garden inhabited by Lucifer must have been a place of extraordinary beauty. It is evident that it constitutes the original plan of God—which He had in mind when He created "the heavens and the earth." It so seems that the garden where Adam and his wife, Eve, lived—and we also will inhabit—is only a replacement, a temporary habitation that has to be destroyed by fire (2 Peter 3:12–13) so that a return to God's original plan may take place. The description of the New Jerusalem offers practically a parallel passage to the one we read in Ezekiel 28.

"And the material of the wall was jasper; and the city was pure gold, like clear glass. The foundation stones of the city wall were adorned with every kind of precious stone. The first foundation stone was jasper; the second, sapphire; the third, chalcedony; the fourth, emerald; the fifth, sardonyx; the sixth, sardius; the seventh, chrysolite; the eighth, beryl; the ninth, topaz; the tenth, chrysoprase; the eleventh, jacinth; the twelfth, amethyst. And the twelve gates were twelve pearls; each one of the gates was a single pearl. And the street of the city was pure gold, like transparent glass" (Revelation 21:18–21).

CHARACTERISTICS OF "ETERNITY PAST"
(Figure 2.1)

During the period we call *eternity past,* which goes from the beginning when God created the heavens and the earth, until that traumatic time in which there was iniquity, rebellion, sin and judgment, there could have passed hundreds, thousands or millions of years; we simply do not know. Time did not mean anything during that period; it was eternity.

The beauty that characterized that creation of God was sublime. But its value does not emanate from its physical beauty but from the fact that during that time all creation operated in harmony. As follows are precisely the two characteristics that made this a perfect epoch:

Only one Authority existed in all creation: God's authority.

There was only one Will in all of creation: the will of the Creator.

In this eternal period God manifested himself exercising His will and authority through that perfect being called Lucifer. Donald Grey Barnhouse says, "The chief of all created beings was set in the government of God as ruler over the creation of God."[12] "Before his fall he may be said to have occupied the role of prime minister for God, ruling possibly over the universe but certainly over this world."[13] He was in charge of exercising the delegated authority of God over all creation (Isaiah 14:16).

God's creation functioned perfectly because everything was an extension of His will and authority. As I said before, this could have lasted centuries, or thousands of years. But then there was a moment when everything changed. The rupture took place

Characteristics of the "Past Eternity"

ETERNITY

GENESIS 1:1
ISAIAH 45:18
EZEKIEL 28:12–15

EDEN

MINERAL BEAUTY

ONLY ONE WILL

THE AUTHORITY
OF GOD

(Figure 2.1)

because rebellion made its entry into creation; there was a manifestation (for the first time in eternity) of a "second will."

THE ORIGIN OF SIN

"You were perfect in your ways from the day you were created, *till iniquity was found in you. By the abundance of your trading you became filled with violence within, and you sinned.*"

> "*Your heart was lifted up because of your beauty;* you corrupted your wisdom *for the sake of your splendor . . . You defiled your sanctuaries by the multitude of your iniquities, by the iniquity of your trading*" (Ezekiel 28:15–18, NKJV).

Let us review before going on.

We had a perfect being who ruled over God's creation, and who exercised the function of a priest. We could say he practically had the function of the high priest of creation. Let's remember the revealing detail of "his sanctuaries." He received the delegation of God's authority, and had praise and worship in his own being (Ezekiel 28:13).

All of God's creation operated perfectly under Lucifer's government until, because of the multitude of his trade, he was filled with iniquity and he sinned. This is the first time sin appears in God's perfect creation.

Verse 16 of the Revised Webster Bible (1995) reads, "by the iniquity of thy merchandise." I have studied this theme thoroughly and have found various synonyms: contracts, trade, trading, transactions, traffic, and commerce. These words suggest exchange.[14]

Trade is exchange. I give a certain amount of money to obtain the product I want. In a store, the cashier receives the money and gives me what I have purchased; there is traffic, there is a transaction, and there is a contract.

When we speak of exchange, we speak of merchandise. And I ask, "What merchandise can be the object of commerce or Lucifer's transactions? What possible exchange could take place between the Creator and his creation?"

Grey Barnhouse states that the merchandise consisted of the authority of God, and the worship of the universe of created creatures towards the Creator.

Because of his position in the holy mountain of God, we understand that Lucifer had the place of maximum authority over creation. On the other hand, we already made reference to the idea of praise and worship because of the words "sanctuaries," "tambourines," and "flutes."

We conclude, then, that while Lucifer exercised the exchange suitable to his priesthood, he received delegated authority from God and he exercised it over the rest of creation. At the same time, he administered the worship that was offered to the Creator.[15] The moment came in which, "[his] heart was lifted up because of [his] beauty; [he] corrupted [his] wisdom for the sake of [his] splendor . . . [He] defiled [his] sanctuaries by the multitude of [his] iniquities, by the iniquity of [his] trading." There came a moment in which, being uplifted, he desired the worship that belongs only to God for himself and usurping God's authority, he took it. In his heart a desire rose—a will that was different from the divine will. Undoubtedly, he even believed he could take God's place. Forgetting his condition of created being, he had the ambition of being as The Creator.

Evidence that this took place comes from the Word of God:

"How you are fallen from heaven, O morning star, son of the dawn! You have been cast down to the earth, you who once laid low the nations! *You said in your heart, 'I will ascend to heaven; I will raise my throne above the stars of God; I will sit enthroned on the mount of assembly, on the utmost heights of the sacred mountain. I will ascend above the tops of the clouds; I will make myself like the Most High'*" (Isaiah 14:12–14, NIV).

In this very decisive moment, many things happen simultaneously *(Figure 2.2)*. Lucifer conspires to take God's place.[16] He is filled with iniquity and he sins. For that reason God casts him out of His holy mountain. But in another action, far more important than Lucifer's individual sin, what happens for the first time in eternity is the manifestation of an additional will to God's will. Nobody had ever dared defy the will of the Creator. In this instant, creation enters into an absolutely different stage. *Now there are two wills in the universe.* Actually, I do not like to speak of two wills, because that it is not absolutely correct. In fact, there was still only one authentic, genuine will, God's. The second is in fact rebellion, rebelliousness, or usurpation.

When the defiance against God's authority takes place, the very harmony of the pre-Adamic creation, which functioned in a perfect way, breaks, thus opening the door for divine judgment at the same time that Lucifer becomes the object of God's wrath.

"Nevertheless you will be thrust down to Sheol, to the recesses of the pit. Those who see you will gaze at you, they will ponder over you, saying, 'Is this the man who made the earth tremble, who shook kingdoms, who made the world like a wilderness and overthrew its cities, who did not allow his prisoners to go home?'" (Isaiah 14:15–17).

In his sin, Lucifer conspired, recruiting a number of the

THE ORIGIN OF SPIRITUAL WARFARE

ETERNITY

GENESIS 1:1 **ISAIAH 45:18** **EZEKIEL 28:12–15**	**ISAIAH 14:12, 20–23** **JEREMIAH 4:23–38** **GENESIS 1:2** **EZEKIEL 28:15–19**
	THE EARTH WAS WITHOUT FORM AND VOID
EDEN	**WHY?** **BECAUSE OF THE RISE OF** • **REBELLION** • **USURPATION** • **CHALLENGE TO THE AUTHORITY**
MINERAL BEAUTY	
ONLY ONE WILL **THE AUTHORITY OF GOD**	**A SECOND WILL**

(Figure 2.2)

God-created beings (Revelation 12:1–12). When God's judgement came, He could have destroyed Satan and these beings that rebelled with him, but He did not do it. Instead, He decided to allow God's creation—which witnessed the rebellion—to also see its consequences. And to defeat Lucifer, now converted into Satan, God in His wisdom chose a creature called *man.*

THE DIVINE JUDGMENT

The judgment of God was released upon all creation. Evidence of the catastrophe of that judgment is found in Jeremiah 4:23–25, RSV, which says (remember that God had created a perfect earth): "I looked on the earth, and lo, it was *waste and void;* and to the heavens, and they had no light. I looked on the mountains, and lo, they were quaking, and all the hills moved to and fro. I looked, and lo, there was no man, and all the birds of the air had fled. I looked, and lo, the fruitful land was a desert, and all its cities were laid in ruins before the LORD, before His fierce anger. For thus says the LORD, 'The whole land shall be a desolation; yet I will not make a full end. For this the earth shall mourn, and the heavens above be black; for I have spoken, I have purposed; I have not relented nor will I turn back.'"

The New American Standard Bible says, "I looked on the earth, and behold, it was *formless and void;* and to the heavens, and they had no light." I hope it is obvious for the reader that God is speaking of the same phrase found in Genesis 1:2.[17]

The apostle Peter adds, "They deliberately ignore this fact, that by the word of God heavens existed long ago, and an earth formed out of water and by means of water, through which *the world that then existed was deluged with water and perished.* But by the same word the heavens and earth *that now exist* have been stored up for fire, being kept until the day of judgment and destruction of ungodly men" (2 Peter 3:5–7, RSV). The Apostle clearly establishes a distinction between the "world that then existed" that was deluged with water and perished, and "the heavens and earth that now exist," stored up for fire until the day of judgment. To believe that this refers to the deluge of the time of Noah makes no sense, because in that opportunity the world did not perish completely.

According to the apostle Peter, the world that then existed was deluged, completely covered with water. Genesis 1:6–8 gives us an account of the second day of creation: "And God said, 'Let there be an expanse between the waters to separate water from water.' So God made the expanse and separated the water under the expanse from the water above it. And it was so. God called the expanse *sky*. And there was evening and there was morning—the second day." According to the Word, the first day, light was created and separated from darkness. Where did that water that covered the heavens and the earth—which had to be separated in two expansions—come from if not from the judgment spoken by Peter?

THE GREAT PARENTHESIS

Due to the rebellion and judgment of Lucifer, a degenerative process of an unknown length for us was produced in him. Certainly, it must have been a long period of darkness, to allow him—who was the seal of perfection—to corrupt until he became Satan, the enemy of God. What a sense of incapability Satan must have experienced when he realized that without God he did not have any creative ability, any possibility of doing anything to prevent the chaotic state in which creation had been left due to his rebellion. "The earth was without form and void, and darkness was upon the face of the deep; and the Spirit of God was moving over the face of the waters" (Genesis 1:2, RSV).

This is the moment in which God decides to end the eternity stage, and He interrupts it by opening a parenthesis that we will call *the times of the Bible (Figure 2.3)*.

God intervenes with the power of His Word, and with only one phrase ends the stage of darkness. "And God said, 'Let there be light'; and there was light. And God saw that the light was good; and God separated the light from the darkness" (Genesis 1:3–4, RSV).

With this Scripture, the week consisting of six work days and one day of rest in which God "fixed" His creation began. Some call this week the re-creation week or second creation. During this time, the seas, trees, grass, sun, stars, and the other natural elements that are so familiar to us make their appearance. This is the Eden we are accustomed to.

Imagine that in the middle of all this operation, the beings that had been judged by God run bewildered from one place to another, witnessing the new creation being displayed before them, when suddenly God says, "Let Us make man in Our image, in Our likeness." That foul being, the devil, listens and says, "Do what?" And the others answer him, "He said, 'man.'" "What is 'man'? Find out what is a 'man.'" But nobody knows. Only God has the answer.

If the devil was already a being full of bitterness and jealousy, at this moment he was consumed with them. He said, "Is God going to make someone according to His image, according to His likeness? How can this being be if I am the seal of perfection?"

In a master act of mercy and infinite wisdom, God designed a perfect plan in which He created a creature a little lower than the angels (Psalm 8:5), to occupy a position of dominion.

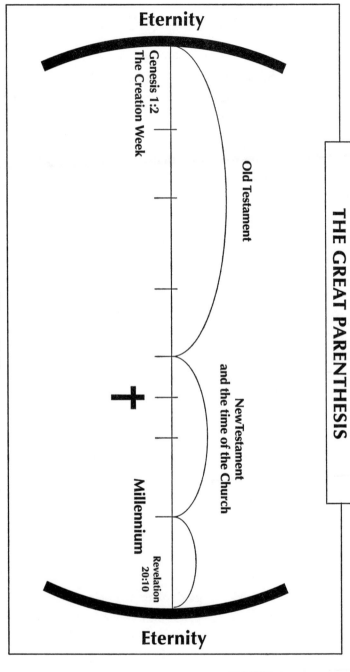

(Figure 2.3)

"Then God said, 'Let Us make man in Our image, in Our like-ness; and let them have dominion over the fish of the sea, and over the fowl of the air, and over the cattle, and over all the earth and over every creeping thing that creepeth upon the earth.'" So God created man in His own image, in the image of God created He him; male and female created He them. And God blessed them, and God said unto them, 'Be fruitful and multiply, and replenish the earth, and subdue it; and have dominion over the fish of the sea, and over the fowl of the air, and over every living thing that moveth upon the earth'" (Genesis 1:26–28, RSV).

As if this was not enough, Jesus tells the Church, "Behold, I have given you authority to tread upon serpents and scorpions, and over all the power of the enemy, and nothing shall injure you" (Luke 10:19).

THE CONTENTS OF THE GREAT PARENTHESIS, "THE TIMES OF THE BIBLE"

The chronology of the great parenthesis begins the day God says: "Let there be light." From there on, as we said before, there is a one-week time span. This is part of the Old Testament, the division that lasts around four thousand years, until the birth of Jesus Christ. Then, the second great division of the Bible, the New Testament, and the subsequent time to the New Testament—the era in which we live—we will call the time of the Church. This period lasts approximately two thousand more years and takes us right to the millennium. At the end of these one thousand years of peace, there is a period of time in which the devil is set loose from his prison, coming out of it to deceive the nations . . . (Revelation 20:7–8). After this, God's temporal plan reaches its grand finale.

"Then comes the end, when He delivers up the kingdom to the God and Father, when He has abolished all rule and all authority and power. For He must reign until He has put all His enemies under His feet. The last enemy that will be abolished is death, for He has put all things in subjection under His feet. When He says, 'All things are put in subjection,' it is evident that He is exempt who put all things in subjection to Him. And when all things are subjected to Him, then the Son Himself also will be subjected to the One who subjected all things to Him, that God may be all in all" (1 Corinthians 15:24–28).

This scripture indicates the end of spiritual warfare; the final moment of the conflict. This will be the day in which Christ will have conquered each one of His enemies, putting them under His feet. All His enemies having perished (Revelation 20:9), the expression of a rebellion will also perish.

"And swore by Him living forever and ever, who created the heaven and the things in it, and the earth and the things in it, and the sea and the things in it, *that time shall no longer be*" (Revelation 10:6, Green's Literal Translation).

To say that time shall no longer be does not mean that time will finish, but that the concept of temporality itself will not exist anymore.

"And the devil, who deceived them, was cast into the lake of fire and brimstone where the beast and the false prophet are. And they will be tormented day and night *forever and ever*" (Revelation 20:10, NKJV).

This is the glorious way in which God announces the end of an era and the great entrance to the following eternity. "Forever and ever" marks the return to eternity where a second will, or a usurped authority, does not exist. The purposes of God have been fulfilled and everything comes back to be the perfect creation of

God, where His children reign upon the earth as kings and priests for God (Revelation 1:6; 5:10) *(Figure 2.4).*

Then *I saw* a new heaven and a new earth; for the first heaven and the first earth had passed away, *and the sea was no more. And I saw the holy city, new Jerusalem, coming down out of heaven from God, prepared as a bride adorned for her husband; and I heard a loud voice from the throne saying, "Behold, the dwelling of God is with men. He will dwell with them, and they shall be His people, and God himself will be with them; He will wipe away every tear from their eyes, and* death shall be no more, neither shall there be mourning nor crying nor pain any more, for the former things have passed away." And He who sat upon the throne said, "Behold, I make all things new." *Also He said, "Write this, for these words are trustworthy and true." And He said to me, "It is done! I am the Alpha and the Omega, the beginning and the end. To the thirsty I will give from the fountain of the water of life without payment. He who conquers shall have this heritage, and I will be his God and he shall be my son. But as for the cowardly, the faithless, the polluted, as for murderers, for-nicators, sorcerers, idolaters, and all liars, their lot shall be in the lake that burns with fire and sulphur, which is the second death." Then came one of the seven angels who had the seven bowls full of the seven last plagues, and spoke to me, saying, "Come, I will show you the Bride, the wife of the Lamb." And in the Spirit he carried me away to a great, high mountain, and showed me the holy city Jerusalem coming down out of heaven from God, having the glory of God, its radiance like a most rare jewel, like a jasper, clear as crystal. It had a great, high wall, with twelve gates, and at the gates twelve angels, and on the gates the names of the twelve tribes of the sons of Israel were inscribed; on the east three gates,*

THE ORIGIN OF SPIRITUAL WARFARE

ETERNITY

Revelation 21:1–27
Revelation 22:1–5
NEW JERUSALEM

Revelation 20:10
1 CORINTHIANS
15:24–26

MINERAL BEAUTY

ONLY ONE WILL

THE AUTHORITY
OF GOD

(Figure 2.4)

on the north three gates, on the south three gates, and on the west three gates. And the wall of the city had twelve foundations, and on them the twelve names of the twelve apostles of the Lamb. And he who talked to me had a measuring rod of gold to measure the city and its gates and walls. The city lies foursquare, its length the same as its breadth; and he measured the city with his rod, twelve thousand stadia; its length and breadth and height are equal. He also measured its wall, a hundred and forty-four cubits by a man's measure, that is, an angel's. The wall was built of jasper, while the city was pure gold, clear as glass. The foundations of the wall of the city were adorned with every jewel; the first was jasper, the second sapphire, the third agate, the fourth emerald, the fifth onyx, the sixth carnelian, the seventh chrysolite, the eighth beryl, the ninth topaz, the tenth chrysoprase, the eleventh jacinth, the twelfth amethyst. And the twelve gates were twelve pearls, each of the gates made of a single pearl, and the street of the city was pure gold, transparent as glass. And I saw no temple in the city, for its temple is the Lord God the Almighty and the Lamb. And the city has no need of sun or moon to shine upon it, for the glory of God is its light, and its lamp is the Lamb. By its light shall the nations walk; and the kings of the earth shall bring their glory into it, and its gates shall never be shut by day—and there shall be no night there; they shall bring into it the glory and the honor of the nations. But nothing unclean shall enter it, nor any one who practices abomination or falsehood, but only those who are written in the Lamb's book of life. Then he showed me the river of the water of life, bright as crystal, flowing from the throne of God and of the Lamb through the middle of the street of the city; also, on either side of the river, the tree of life with its twelve kinds of fruit, yielding its fruit each month; and the leaves of the tree were for the healing of the nations. There shall no more be anything accursed, *but the*

throne of God and of the Lamb shall be in it, and his servants shall
worship him; they shall see his face, and his name shall be on their
foreheads. And night shall be no more; they need no light of lamp
or sun, for the Lord God will be their light, and they shall reign
for ever and ever.

Revelation 21:1–22:5, RSV

The history of God's creation consists then of an eternity—interrupted by a temporal parenthesis—where the human being has to
confront evil.

Paul E. Billheimer, in his book, *Destined to Overcome,*[18] suggests that in God's wisdom, our passing through this world, and
the confrontation against the forces of evil, is truly for our training to reign with Him for eternity.

Once this parenthesis ends, things will come back to their original state: an eternity where God rules with one single will, one only
divine authority, and one beautiful kingdom—of eminently mineral nature—in which the children of God will live forever and ever.

CHARACTERISTICS OF "THE TIMES
OF THE BIBLE" *(Figure 2.5)*

Because our lot has been to live in the times in which two wills
coexist, the basic characteristic of the world in which we live is
dichotomy, dualism, and duality.[19]

For us, it is very natural that there is good and evil, black and
white, north and south, cold and hot. We experience this duality
in all areas of life. Before us there is always a double possibility,
two roads; the narrow road and the broad road; we can go to the
north or to the south; to the right or to the left. There is always
before us an alternative, a fork in the road.

THE ORIGIN OF SPIRITUAL WARFARE

"The Times of the Bible"

TIME

The Interval Between the Two Eternities

The Re-Creation Week Genesis 1:3
Man is created Genesis 1:26–27
Fall of man

Revelation 10:10

Genesis 1:2

Old Testament   New Testament

Post
New Testament
Time

Millennium

The Marriage
Revelation 19:7–9

TWO WILLS
☐ ONE WILL (GOD'S)
☐ ONE REBELLION (SATAN'S)

Dualism
Dichotomy
Duality

Good - Bad
North - South
Cold - Hot
Blessing - Curse
Tree of Life - Tree of the knowledge
of good and evil

ETERNITY

Revelation 21:1–27

Revelation 22:1–5

New Jersualem

Mineral Beauty

ONLY ONE WILL

ETERNITY

Genesis 1:1
Isaiah 45:18
Exekiel 28:12–15

EDEN

Mineral Beauty

ONLY ONE WILL

(*Figure 2.5*)

For this reason there were two trees in the garden. The existence of two options was necessary so that the exercise of free will would be possible. God does not desire to have a robot. God wants to have a Church that will voluntarily choose to love, adore, and follow His will. Together with the two trees, a word that was unknown makes its entrance: Death. "But you must not eat from the tree of the knowledge of good and evil, for when you eat of it you will surely die" (Genesis 2:17, NIV).

If the readers are careful, they will notice that one of those two trees, the tree of life, that represents the will of God, is preserved, and it appears again in the eternal future. "And on either side of the river was the tree of life" (Revelation 22:2a). But the tree of the knowledge of good and evil never appears again.

Time and time again we hear, jokingly, that it was an apple tree. I think that this argument has a satanic origin, because it makes something that God definitely prohibited appear innocent. If eating from the tree of life would produce man to live forever (Genesis 3:22), it is natural to assume that the tree of the knowledge of good and evil would produce exactly that: knowledge of good and evil.

When God said to man, "but you must not eat of the tree of the knowledge of good and evil, for when you eat of it you will surely die" (Genesis 2:17, NIV), He referred to the fact that the knowledge of good and evil had in itself a seed that would bring death to man. Physical death? No, spiritual death—separation from God. Let's notice that Adam ate, and yet he lived many years after that. But he lived them separated from the communion with God that he had once enjoyed. This is similar to what happens to all who seek after knowledge in the occult, sects, divination, etc. As a matter of fact, I believe that the knowledge of good was already something man possessed. He already knew God. What surely would harm him, would be the knowledge of evil.

Therefore, now, two wills exist, there are two trees in the garden, and dualism is present everywhere. What is to come is the next logical step. There are two kingdoms: the kingdom of God, and the kingdom of darkness (Luke 11:18). In the next chapter we will study the interaction of the believer with both kingdoms and will discover how the human being is the central character in the conflict we call spiritual warfare *(Figure 2.6)*.

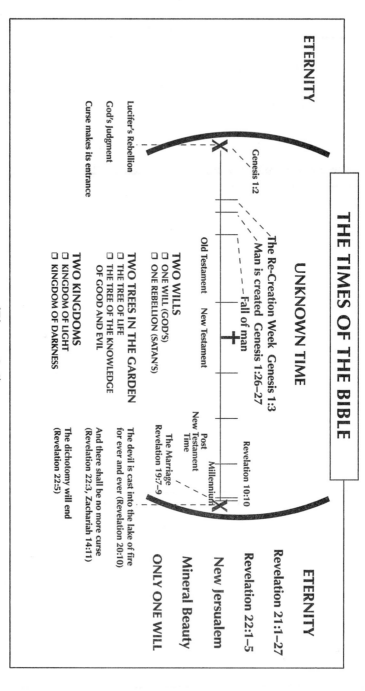

(*Figure 2.6*)

4

Participation of Man in the Conflict

Thy kingdom come. Thy will be done, on earth as it is in heaven.

MATTHEW 6:10

When the devil noticed that a new being existed, created in the image and likeness of God, destined to have the lordship over creation, he developed his own plan and wanted to destroy God's work. Satan's attack consisted in tempting Adam and Eve with exactly the same iniquity that constituted his own ruin. Lucifer himself had wanted to be like God. That was what he offered Eve, saying, "You will not surely die . . . For God knows that when you eat of it your eyes will be opened, and you will be like God, knowing good and evil" (Genesis 3:4,5 NIV). How ironic! This is the weapon he used against Eve, as it is the one he still primarily uses with humanism, in which he convinces man there is no God but rather that man himself is the center of the universe. His most recent strategy has been called the New Age, whose watchword is, "There will come a time in which, through enlightenment, you will become gods." Indeed, such a new age does not exist. It is the same old lie of the devil.

The teaching that we can extract from the temptation and fall of man is a primary key to understanding spiritual warfare.

The Bible states with absolute clarity that Eve, being deceived, incurred transgression (see 1 Timothy 2:13). *Transgress* means "to break or violate a precept, law, or statute." This is what we call disobedience. In the second Eden there was a tree of which it was prohibited to partake. That is precisely what Adam and Eve did. They voluntarily decided to violate the prohibition, acting without taking the will of God into account.

In other words, Adam and Eve made a voluntary decision. They chose to reject the will of God and adopt the "other will." When they decided to ally themselves with the will of the devil, they became rebels with him, and thus committed treason against God, giving Satan the place of lordship God had entrusted to them. The devil became the prince of this world, the prince of the power of the air and god of this age (John 14:30, Ephesians 2:2 and 2 Corinthians 4:4).

THE "WORLD" SYSTEM

The word *kosmos,* which is translated "world" in the Bible, speaks of a system of social order, a complex set of "orders and structures"[20] that sustain life in society. Because of the word in 2 Peter 3:6 we know that there was a social order that expired, and another that subsists today. This world that is in force, its conditions and its future, have great importance to our study.

The Word is very clear. In its origin, all things were made "good."

"He is the image of the invisible God, the firstborn over all creation. For by him all things were created: things in heaven and on earth, visible and invisible, whether thrones or powers or rulers or authorities; all things were created by him and for him" (Colossians 1:15,16, NIV).

"And God saw all that He had made, and behold, it was very good" (Genesis 1:31).

From the instant in which two wills existed, the system was already different. Furthermore, when man chose to renounce the will of God, to take the road of rebellion, eating from the fruit of the prohibited tree, everything changed. The knowledge of good and evil made its entrance. Man now had a knowledge that corrupted him, poisoned him. Adam, who once was created in the image and likeness of God, now reproduced himself in his fallen state. "When Adam had lived 130 years, he had a son *in his own likeness, in his own image;* and he named him Seth" (Genesis 5:3, NIV). Now humanity carries in itself the seed of evil (see Romans 8:21–24) that it transmits from generation to generation. "Therefore, just as through one man sin entered into the world, and death through sin, and so death spread to all men, because all sinned . . ." (Romans 5:12).

In the moment in which the devil enters into a place of authority over man and creation, the polluted and corrupt world becomes his vehicle of expression, a system designed to keep humanity in slavery (see John 12:31 and Ephesians 2:2). The Bible teaches us that since then, the world serves the devil's purposes.

"We know that we are children of God, and that the whole world is under the control of the evil one" (1 John 5:19, NIV).

For that reason, a person who is not renewed, a natural person, finds his environment or natural habitat in the world, but a believer is a foreigner in the world.

John 17:14–16 says, "I have given them Thy word; and the world has hated them, because they are not of the world, even as

I am not of the world. I do not ask Thee to take them out of the world, but to keep them from the evil one. *They are not of the world,* even as I am not of the world."

There we were enslaved until we were caught away, rescued and brought to the Kingdom of God (Colossians 1:13).

"So also we, while we were children, were held in bondage under the elemental things of the world" (Galatians 4:3).

However, the proof that the world is a set of complex structures designed to trap humanity and keep it captive (2 Corinthians 4:4) is that God shows us that an already delivered believer risks being captured again by the structures of the world system.

Galatians 4:9 says, "But now that you have come to know God, or rather to be known by God, how is it that you turn back again to the weak and worthless elemental things, to which you desire to be enslaved all over again?"

I am convinced that believers in general ignore the severity of this subject. The world is a polluted system that has the power to enslave human beings through their way of thinking. When we study the *strongholds* we will understand the true reaches of this complex system of orders and invisible structures.

"See to it that no one takes you captive through philosophy and empty deception, according to the tradition of men, according to the elementary principles of the world, rather than according to Christ" (Colossians 2:8).

A REVEALING DREAM

I am very grateful to God because He has revealed most of the material you are reading to me in His mercy and compassion. It is true that I have studied the subject. I have a library that, when Dr. Peter Wagner came to my house and saw it, he exclaimed,

"Your library of spiritual warfare is larger than mine!" However, I give credit to the love of God and His supernatural intervention for much of the material we are studying.

One Saturday night, after having finished preparing for the next day, I went to bed. I had the Sunday message ready, I had prayed and I felt my rest would be normal.

At midnight, I had an extraordinary dream, in which I felt God's presence and I heard His voice. "Tonight, I want us to do something special. I am going to quiz you." Suddenly, a very large screen came down, while I heard the first question. "How many sources of power are there in the universe?" I responded with another question, "Sources of power?" The Lord assented. "Yes, tell me, who has power in the universe?" I said, "You, of course, Lord God."

Somehow, I could write in that screen as if it were a blackboard *(Figure 3.1)*. I wrote in the upper left side corner, like this, with capital letters, GOD. I said, "You, Father, are the source of power; You are the Almighty," and of course, I wrote there, Father, Son and Holy Spirit.

I do not believe it necessary to quote the scriptures that demonstrate that God is the Almighty. He is the only Creator of the heavens and the earth. Then, God told me, "All right, show me another source that generates power."

"All right," I answered, and wrote further down in lower case letters, the devil.

God asked, "The devil?" I answered, "Yes, Lord, the devil has power; or doesn't he have power?" He answered, making me write a list of Scriptures: Revelation 1:18, Matthew 28:18, Colossians 2:15 and Hebrews 2:14 *(Figure 3.2)*. I continued writing what He dictated to me, when He said, "Read those verses to Me."

I, intrigued, obeyed. Then I read the scripture where God

THE SOURCES OF POWER

GOD

Father

Son

Holy Spirit

(Figure 3.1)

says, I am "the living One; and I was dead, and behold, I am alive forevermore, and I have the keys of death and of Hades" (Revelation 1:18). Then, the Lord told me, "What do you understand?" I responded "Jesus says that He is who lives and was dead, who is alive forevermore and has the keys of death and of Hades." The Lord interrupted me, "Who has the keys?" I answered, "Jesus has them. Yes, Lord, Jesus has them." "Then, what keys does the devil have?" asked the Lord. I had to recognize, "He does not have keys; because if Jesus has them, the devil cannot have them."

Then the Lord proceeded, "Read Matthew 28:18 to me," and I said, "You know it, Lord. It is Jesus Christ again, who speaks saying, "All authority has been given to Me in heaven and on earth." After He had me repeat it, He asked me, "What power does the devil have?" "None, because it is Jesus Christ who has all power, in heaven and in earth." In that moment, my heart started to understand what He purposed to teach me.

And then he proposed, "Why don't you read Colossians 2:15 to me?"

"When He had disarmed the rulers and authorities, He made a public display of them, having triumphed over them through Him." "What power does the devil have? And the principalities? And the powers?" asked the Lord. "They do not have any kind of power. Jesus stripped them of all power," I answered.

At last, the Lord said, "Read Hebrews 2:14 to me." Once more, the scripture referred to the work of Christ. "Since then the children share in flesh and blood, He Himself likewise also partook of the same, *that through death He might render powerless him who had the power of death, that is, the devil.*" Through His sacrifice, Christ condemns the devil[21] and closes the door that Adam had opened.[22]

"Then," He asked again, "what power does the devil have?"

GOD

Father

Son

Holy Spirit

The devil

Revelation 1:18
Matthew 28:18
Colossians 2:15
Hebrews 2:14

(Figure 3.2)

While I marked with a large letter X the word *devil,* I responded, "None, Lord, none." (*Figure 3.3)*

I ask you, please, to stop for a moment and analyze. God has power. He is a source that generates power. The devil doesn't have any power because it was taken from him. Settle this in your heart:

1. The devil does not have power because he does not have any keys.

2. The Word of God says he has no power.

3. He was stripped and exhibited in public.

4. He was destroyed, annulled or rendered powerless.

Immediately after, God proceeded to draw three concentric circles in the middle of the screen, and He ordered me to write over them, *Man.* In that instant, I understood what this was all about, because I am accustomed to using those three circles to describe the division of man in three parts; spirit, soul and body (1 Thessalonians 5:23). When I saw the screen, I understood that it was a list of the beings in the universe. Deity was in the upper left side, the devil (and undoubtedly his demons) in the lower right side, and at the center, Man. *(Figure 3.4)*

After that, God, signaling the exterior circle that symbolizes the body, asked, "Does the human body have power?" My answer came right away, "No, Lord, of course not. It is a biblical and scientific fact that the human body wears down day by day" (2 Corinthians 4:16).

Then He proceeded, "And what about the spirit of man; does it have power?" I answered, "Well . . . yes and no." I answered in that way because he certainly has the power of the born-again

GOD

Father

Son

Holy Spirit

The Devil

Revelation 1:18

Matthew 28:18

Colossians 2:15

Hebrews 2:14

(Figure 3.3)

man, but it is the power of the Holy Spirit, not of the human spirit. In other words, it is not another source of power but the same that we included in the Deity section, Father, Son, and *Holy Spirit*. If we speak of a man that does not know God, we cannot talk about him as the temple of the Spirit of the Lord.

The time for the last question came and it was this: "Son, what are we left with?" I answered, "The soul of man, Lord."

I concluded that the soul of man is the only alternative source of power in the universe. The soul of man has power, the power of deciding what to do with the lordship or authority that the Lord gave it.

You see, dear reader, the soul of the human being has three parts: mind, emotions and will. Let us stop here for a moment and remember that man is the only being created in the image and likeness of God. Man is the only one that has the capacity to think because he has a mind, the capacity to feel because he has emotions and the capacity to decide because he has a will. These three characteristics constitute what we call free will. Let us dwell on this concept for a moment. God, the Creator, voluntarily decided to make a human being in His image and likeness and gave him the capacity to make his own decisions. He gave him the ability of thinking, feeling, and speaking; but above all, to decide and act. He put him in the garden of Eden, the second Eden, and gave him lordship over all that was created (Genesis 1:28), even though God knew that two wills exist, one that is genuine and one that is rebellious. The power of decision in man will incline him to one or the other. The consequences of his decisions will incline the balance to one kingdom or the other. The human being is the only additional source of "lordship" or authority because God gave it to him. He delegated it to him.

GOD

Father

Son

Holy Spirit

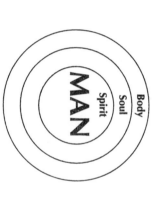

The Devil

Revelation 1:18

Matthew 28:18

Colossians 2:15

Hebrews 2:14

(*Figure 3.4*)

Coming back to our most important question: If the devil has no power, why is it that we see him exercising it? The answer is very delicate. It would be very naïve to think that the devil can use the power of God. Then, which one is left? The power that the devil uses is the one that comes from the soul of men.

THE POWER OF THE SOUL OF MEN
(Figure 3.5)

All the time there is a disjunctive before us, a duality, a dichotomy: good or evil, north or south, positive or negative, hot or cold. Even believers have to make decisions in the middle of duality. They choose to walk in the flesh or walk in the sprit, live by faith or live by what is seen, walk in the law of sin and death or walk in the law of the spirit of life in Christ Jesus. All of this is duality. We continually confront two possibilities, road A or road B. All of our actions depend on one decision before that dual disjunctive. There is not a single moment we can escape from a double possibility. We can go to side A or we can go to side B.

Now, remember the tree of life. When Adam and Eve stood before the tree, they had two possibilities. They could obey or disobey. Side A was the side of obedience, the side of the will of God. Side A represented total dependence on God. To obey the commandment would have meant obedience and faithfulness to God. On the contrary, side B meant disobedience to God, and with it, faithfulness to the kingdom of darkness.

I am very interested in making a special note on the importance of the word *faithfulness,* because at the end of the Bible, the purpose of God is disclosed. He desired a people for Himself, a people of kings and priests. It was called Israel in the Old Testament; it is called the Church in the New Testament, and it

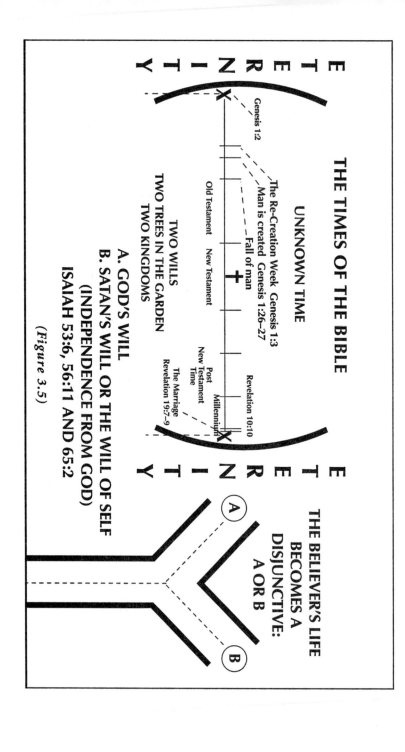

THE TIMES OF THE BIBLE

UNKNOWN TIME

Genesis 1:2

The Re-Creation Week Genesis 1:3
Man is created Genesis 1:26–27
Fall of man

Old Testament   New Testament

Revelation 10:10

Post
New Testament
Time

The Marriage
Revelation 19:7–9

Millennium

TWO WILLS
TWO TREES IN THE GARDEN
TWO KINGDOMS

A. GOD'S WILL
B. SATAN'S WILL OR THE WILL OF SELF
(INDEPENDENCE FROM GOD)
ISAIAH 53:6, 56:11 AND 65:2

THE BELIEVER'S LIFE
BECOMES A
DISJUNCTIVE:
A OR B

Ⓐ

Ⓑ

(*Figure 3.5*)

will be called the bride of the Lamb in eternity. This means that this entire plan will be fulfilled when there is a "wife." It draws my attention. What is the quality of a wife? Faithfulness.

On the contrary, the devil finishes his plan with a "great harlot." What is the quality or characteristic of a prostitute? Unfaithfulness. This means that the destiny of the human being is to become the bride of Christ through obedience or be part of the great harlot through disobedience.

Here is where the power of the soul of men is actually exercised. Man, through his free will, decides his future. I must bring your attention to the fact that God's respect for our free will is so great that He does not impose His salvation on anyone, but He will respect the one who rejects Him and will let him pass into eternal condemnation (Mark 16:16). Now I will submit to your consideration a very powerful reasoning:

A) What man does depends on what he decides.

That means that the first process in us is to make a decision. "Yes, we are going to the service tonight." "No, we will not go to the service tonight." Before we act, it is necessary to make a decision.

B) What man does determines his alignment with one of the kingdoms.

Each one of the kingdoms has a different purpose. What man decides determines what he does. What he does determines the purpose he contributes to; that is, which kingdom he serves. When I decide to align myself with the kingdom of God, I am faithful to it, I give my loyalty to God, and I submit myself to Him. This is what being dependent on God means. When I do this, I serve His purposes.

However, when I decide to do what I want, what my own

desires dictate to me, when I think I can be my own god and make my own decisions, I go to the other way; the way of independence from God. Because I am independent from God, I do my own will and fall into unfaithfulness and fall into disobedience. Even worse, I fall into rejecting the authority of God.[23]

"And in the generations gone by He permitted all the nations to go their own ways" (Acts 14:16).

C) What man decides and does strengthens the kingdom to which he has given his loyalty.

Men's actions can only be the fruit either of obedience or disobedience to God. Every time a human being obeys God, the impact of his actions reinforces the kingdom of light. For example, if I decide to obey the mandate of praying without ceasing, surely my prayers will have an impact in the spiritual kingdom. If I decide to obey the commandment of preaching the gospel to all creatures, the fruit will be especially effective to the kingdom in which I have professed loyalty.

If I decide to be neutral and do nothing, good or bad—as many do today—I will be wasting the opportunity of serving my Lord. As He said, "He who is not with Me is against Me; and he who does not gather with Me scatters" (Matthew 12:30).

If, on the contrary, I give myself to transgression and sin, I will be contributing to the strengthening of the covering of darkness that is formed by the sin of men.

More than once, believers have asked me, "Are you trying to tell me that I may be contributing to the kingdom of darkness?" Yes, that is exactly what I am saying.

Every time we make a decision based on our own desires, we are being independent from God, and that is equivalent to ignoring His will. When the law of God that is written in you, your heart tells you, "This is not right," and you voluntarily ignore it, persisting in an improper behavior, in that instant you are exercising the source of power God gave you. It is called soul, and sadly, you are putting it to Satan's service.

D) The repetitive and continued action of men determines the spiritual atmosphere over a family, a community or a nation.

Does this mean that the kingdom of darkness is nurtured by the actions of men? Yes, that is exactly what it means. Men's actions close the heavens over us (Deuteronomy 28:23), through the formation of what we call the covering of darkness.

Let me say it this way: The kingdom of Satan is also called the kingdom of darkness. Why? Precisely because that is its nature, in contrast to the kingdom of light. Remember what the Word says through the apostle John:

"In Him was life, and the life was the light of men" (John 1:4).

"And this is the message we have heard from Him and announce to you, that God is light, and in Him there is no darkness at all" (1 John 1:5–7).

You may notice that the Word says that if we walk in the light, as He is in the light, we then have fellowship with one another, and the blood of Jesus, His Son, purifies us from all sin. (See also Acts 17:28.) If on the contrary, we walk in darkness, draw your own conclusions. Now, we do not say this only of those who do not know Christ, but even the actions of believers can make this weaving that we call the covering of darkness grow.[24]

"The one who says he is in the light and yet hates his brother is in the darkness until now" (1 John 2).

LUST (CONCUPISCENCE)

Here, I have to explain that the duality, the disjunctive of which we have spoken, offers two possibilities. The first is to align my will with the will of God and His kingdom. The second has two possibilities in it. One of them consists in aligning my will to Satan's. Very few believers would do that, but the other alternative consists in doing my own will, that, even if it is not Satan's will, is absolutely independent from God.

There are persons who believe that disobeying certain biblical mandates is not that important, or they decide to do things that are not exactly prohibited by God, but that are not pleasing to Him.

The bottom line is determined by two words: dependence and independence. To be dependent on God means voluntarily carrying out His will. To be independent means to do whatever other will is different from God's, be it the devil's or my own.

The will of God is for His children not to be independent from Him but rather, that they imitate Christ who said, "For I have come down from heaven, not to do My own will, but the will of Him who sent Me" (John 6:38).

"And He who sent Me is with Me; He has not left Me alone, for I always do the things that are pleasing to Him" (John 8:29).

"Not everyone who says to Me, 'Lord, Lord,' will enter the kingdom of heaven; but he who does the will of My Father who is in heaven" (Matthew 7:21).

"I can do nothing on My own initiative. As I hear, I judge; and My judgment is just, because I do not seek My own will, but the will of Him who sent Me" (John 5:30).

The Bible says that each one is tempted when, by his own evil desire [lust, concupiscence], he is dragged away and enticed. Let's stop for a moment and think. If life is light, then, what is death? Darkness. Every time sin is committed death is produced. Every time sin is committed darkness is produced. The weaving of which the darkness covering is made up is the result of the wicked actions of men. The search for my own desires is called concupiscence.

"Blessed is a man who perseveres under trial; for once he has been approved, he will receive the crown of life, which the Lord has promised to those who love Him. Let no one say when he is tempted, 'I am being tempted by God'; for God cannot be tempted by evil, and He Himself does not tempt anyone. But each one is tempted when he is carried away and enticed by his own lust. *Then when lust has conceived, it gives birth to sin; and when sin is accomplished, it brings forth death"* (James 1:12–15).

"For by these He has granted to us His precious and magnificent promises, in order that by them you might become partakers of the divine nature, *having escaped the corruption that is in the world by lust"* (2 Peter 1:4).

Why is there corruption in the world? Because of lust. I have the following note, from the Greek, in my Bible, "Because each one wants to pursue its own way." In other words, the world is like it is because men have taken road B instead of road A *(Figure 3.6)* and they have become independent from God instead of dependent on Him.

"All of us like sheep have gone astray, each of us has turned to his own way; but the Lord has caused the iniquity of us all to fall on Him" (Isaiah 53:6).

"And the dogs are greedy, they are not satisfied. And they are shepherds who have no understanding; *They have all turned to their own way, each one to his unjust gain,* to the last one" (Isaiah 56:11).

"I have spread out My hands all day long to a rebellious people, *who walk in the way which is not good, following their own thoughts, a people who continually provoke Me to My face,* offering sacrifices in gardens and burning incense on bricks" (Isaiah 65:2–3).

"You too have done evil, even more than your forefathers;

THE POWER OF MEN'S SOULS

THE BELIEVER'S LIFE BECOMES A DISJUNCTIVE: A OR B

- WHAT MAN DECIDES DETERMINES WHAT HE DOES.

- WHAT MAN DOES DETERMINES HIS ALIGNMENT WITH ONE OF THE TWO KINGDOMS.

- WHAT MAN DECIDES AND DOES REINFORCES THE KINGDOM TO WHICH HE HAS SWORN LOYALTY.

- THE CONTINUED, REPETITIVE ACTION OF MEN DETERMINES THE SPIRITUAL ATMOSPHERE UPON A LIFE, A FAMILY, A CITY OR A NATION.

A. GOD'S WILL
B. SATAN'S WILL OR THE WILL OF SELF
   (INDEPENDENCE FROM GOD)
   ISAIAH 53:6, 56:11 AND 65:2

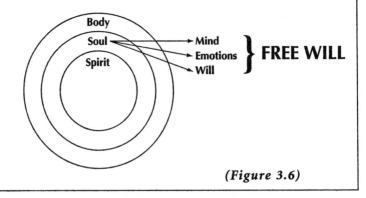

Body
Soul → Mind
Spirit → Emotions
→ Will
} FREE WILL

(Figure 3.6)

for behold, *you are each one walking according to the stubbornness of his own evil heart, without listening to Me"* (Jeremiah 16:12).

The church is facing the great challenge of cleansing its ways, (Jeremiah 15:19, NKJV), so that the manifold wisdom of God might be made known by the church to the principalities and powers in the heavenly places. This way, through spiritual warfare, we will recover the positions that were given to Satan because of human sin. The devil did not have any power to take them from us; we were the ones who gave them to him.

THE DEVIL USES THE POWER OF LUST

Due to the fact that the devil was stripped of all power, the only ability that he can use on us to achieve his purpose is lying. It is his nature. "You are of your father the devil, and you want to do the desires of your father. He was a murderer from the beginning, and does not stand in the truth, because there is no truth in him. Whenever he speaks a lie, he speaks from his own nature; for he is a liar, and the father of lies"(John 8:44).

The devil has a special interest in using the power of the human soul. It is the only resource he can make use of.[25]

Look at the list of merchandise that characterizes the Babylonian commerce:

"And the merchants of the earth will weep and mourn over her, for no one buys their merchandise anymore: merchandise of gold and silver, precious stones and pearls, fine linen and purple, silk and scarlet, every kind of citron wood, every object of ivory, every kind of object of most precious wood, bronze, iron, and marble; and cinnamon and incense, fragrant oil and frankincense, wine and oil, fine flour and wheat, cattle and sheep, horses and chariots, *and bodies [slaves,* NASB] *and souls of men"* (Revelation 18:11–13, NKJV).

The first part of the list is fairly normal, but the final part refers to slaves, souls of men. Of course, the mention of Babylon in this passage corresponds to the kingdom of Lucifer, son of dawn (see Isaiah 14:4,12 and Ezekiel 28:16–19).

That is what the activity of the devil has always been, keeping the human race under bondage (see 2 Corinthians 4:4). That is the reason for our study. Only in this way will we march forward towards the goal of spiritual warfare: evangelism that delivers humanity from the power of darkness to the kingdom of Jesus Christ (Colossians 1:13).

"To open their eyes so that they may turn from darkness to light and from the dominion of Satan to God, in order that they may receive forgiveness of sins and an inheritance among those who have been sanctified by faith in Me'" (Acts 26:18).

Thank God for John's prophecy, which added in the next verse of Scripture that we read:

"And the fruit you long for has gone from you, and all things that were luxurious and splendid have passed away from you and *men will no longer find them"* (Revelation 18:14). A glorious day will come in which the souls of men will no longer serve the devil's purposes, but will serve exclusively the Lord, the only God, the creator of the heavens and the earth.

Let's concentrate for a moment on the techniques of the enemy.

"In order that no advantage be taken of us by Satan; for we are not ignorant of his schemes" (2 Corinthians 2:11).

Today, movements like the New Age movement are fulfilling the prophecy given to John. They are using the souls of people as merchandise. The only power that exists, apart from the power of the Holy Spirit, is the power of the soul.

Let's examine the soul of man. When God created Adam, he created him in his image and likeness. The characteristics of Adam were extraordinary. His spirit had full communion with God, a communion so intimate that there was no need to call upon the name of the Lord (see Genesis 4:26). He had a strong body that enabled him to keep and dress the garden, in spite of its extraordinary dimensions. Remember that the river that came out of the garden separated in four: Pishon, Gihon, Tigris, and the well-known Euphrates. But the area that interests us, the soul of Adam, was so powerful that his mind named all the animals, dominated the earth, and exercised lordship over all the animals of creation. Nevertheless, on the day of the fall, he did not use his authority over the animals, he did not respect the guidance of his spirit, but decided to submit his soul to his flesh, and he was enslaved by that decision.

The scientists explain to us that today, human beings have a great potential. We do not even use ten percent of our mental ability. Why is it we do not use it? Why is it we do not take advantage of it? Because since the fall of man, the power of the soul of man has been submitted to the flesh.

However, the devil knows that this power is there, and he uses it to manifest himself. Probably, this is the reason why unclean spirits are always hunting for a body in which to manifest (see Matthew 12:43–45).

With the objective of extracting that power from man, the devil has originated different religions, spiritist techniques, and even spiritualists. Some examples are, Transcendental Meditation, animism, Hinduism, Buddhism, Shintoism, New Age, etc.

Many of these beliefs find their support in miraculous manifestations that even confuse believers.

There are healings and signs that do not come from God (Acts 8:9–11). There is fortune-telling, which is not prophecy

(Acts 16:16–18). The devil makes people meditate and levitate. A brother, member of the church, told me that before he received Christ, he had been involved in one of these cults, believing that it guided him to the Truth. He learned to levitate, and for that, during his meditation, he had to call upon seven spirits by name. He told me that if he made a mistake in the order, the demons would torment him with very painful chastisements. But if he reached the seventh demon, in the correct order, he would levitate to a height of more than one meter.

We find another example in the concept of the *kundalini* force that the Hindus practice. After performing violent physical exercises during one or two hours, their mind is left totally blank, the serpent that they believe to have in their spine uncoils, and the power of the soul emerges to be used. We have all seen, even if it has been in a cartoon, a *fakir* who lies on a bed of nails or punctures his skin with a knife and does not even bleed. Surely we know of the mentalist who holds a spoon or another metal object and before the eyes of an audience, bends it with the power of the mind. It especially impresses me to see the people who chew and eat glass or "swallow a spade." These are some of the ways in which the devil makes a show of "his" power, which is actually only borrowed power.

The devil uses the power of the human soul as the resource he needs to manifest himself. On the contrary, God does not have any use for the power that proceeds from the soul. God will only use the power that proceeds from the Holy Spirit, and this is what the spirit of the believer does (Ephesians 3:20).

Watchman Nee affirms, about the power of the human soul, that "This power had fallen with man, so that according to God's will it should not be used any further." [26] That is why the Lord Jesus Christ frequently declares that we need to lose our life, that is, the power of the soul, in reference to Matthew 10:39 and 16:25.

Today we see an explosion of cults and religions, because the Scripture declares that "in the latter days . . ." (See 1 Timothy 4:1–3.)

Let's recapitulate. What does the devil wish to achieve? He wants to make use of us, or better said, exploit us. He has wanted to do this from the very moment he was cast down because humans were created in God's image and likeness. Since the second Eden, he presented himself as a serpent in the Garden saying, "I will strip them of their power to challenge God again." That desire will be taken to extreme consequences, as shown in Revelation 20:7–9.

Now, what does God expect from us? He expects that we voluntarily give ourselves over to Him and that we willingly die to ourselves, despising our lives for Him. Only then will we be included among the overcomers.

"He who loves his life loses it; and he who hates his life in this world shall keep it to life eternal" (John 12:25).

"And they overcame him because of the blood of the Lamb and because of the word of their testimony, *and they did not love their life even to death"* (Revelation 12:11).

To him that overcomes, says the Lord Jesus Christ (NIV),

1. I will give the right to eat from the tree of life (Revelation 2:7).

2. He will not be hurt at all by the second death (Revelation 2:11).

3. I will give some of the hidden manna. I will also give him a white stone with a new name written on it, known only to him who receives it (Revelation 2:17).

4. I will give authority over the nations (Revelation 2:26).

5. He will be dressed in white. I will never blot out his name from the book of life, but will acknowledge his name before my Father and His angels (Revelation 3:5).

6. I will make a pillar in the temple of My God. Never again will he leave it. I will write on him the name of My God and the name of the city of My God, . . . and I will also write on him My new name (Revelation 3:12).

7. I will give the right to sit with Me on My throne, just as I overcame and sat down with My Father on His throne (Revelation 3:21).

5

The Kingdoms

The time is fulfilled, and the kingdom of God is at hand;
repent and believe in the gospel.

MARK 1:15

CHARACTERISTICS OF THE KINGDOMS
(Figure 4.1)

We have before us two opposite kingdoms that have their own features.

The features of the kingdom of God are light, truth, and love.

"In Him was life, and the life was the light of men" (John 1:4).

"Jesus said to him, 'I am the way, and the truth, and the life; no one comes to the Father, but through Me'" (John 14:6).

"The one who does not love does not know God, for God is love" (1 John 4:8).

The features of the kingdom of Satan are darkness, lies, and fear.

"And the light shines in the darkness, and the darkness did not comprehend it" (John 1:5).

"You are of your father the devil, and you want to do the desires of your father. He was a murderer from the beginning, and

THE KINGDOMS

~~DOM~~ OF LIGHT	KINGDOM OF DARKNESS
Light – John 1:5	Darkness – John 1:5
Truth – 1 Timothy 2:4	Lie – 1 Timothy 2:4
Love – 1 John 4:8	Fear – 1 John 4:8

CHARACTERISTICS OF THE KINGDOMS

Authentic or Genuine Authority	Rebellion Insurrection

CONSEQUENCES OF INTERACTING WITH THE KINGDOMS

Obedience	Disobedience
Blessing	Curse
Deuteronomy 30:19	Proverbs 26:2

THE LANGUAGE OF THE TWO KINGDOMS

INTERCESSION	INDICTMENT
Hebrews 7:25	Revelation 12:10

(Figure 4.1)

does not stand in the truth, because there is no truth in him. Whenever he speaks a lie, he speaks from his own nature; for he is a liar, and the father of lies" (John 8:44).

"There is no fear in love; but perfect love casts out fear, because fear involves punishment, and the one who fears is not perfected in love" (1 John 4:18).

CONSEQUENCES OF OUR INTERACTION WITH THE KINGDOMS

During the time of the great parenthesis, we constantly interact with both kingdoms. It is somewhat like the law of gravity. It is present all the time. It makes no difference if I see it or not; it is there nonetheless, and I will have to live with its consequences, be they convenient or not. In the same way, my interaction with the kingdoms has consequences. It does not matter if I am aware of them or not. Everything I do generates consequences.

The consequences of my interaction with the kingdoms depend on my attitudes. An attitude of loyalty to the kingdom of God will produce blessing.

I have to affirm here that this truth is valid for those who know Christ and for those who still do not know Him. Many times we see people who do not even believe the Word as we do, and yet receive the blessing that it establishes. Why? Because the interaction with the kingdom *always* produces consequences.

On the other hand, an attitude of loyalty to the kingdom of darkness, which implies disloyalty to the kingdom of God, will provoke a curse.

Probably the best scripture to illustrate this truth is chapter 28 of the book of Deuteronomy, where each consequence of serving the Lord or serving other gods is perfectly described.

The blessings and curses are those invisible, spiritual elements that determine the results in the life of a person.

I have always been intrigued about why a person, a family, or even a nation, that seems to have all natural circumstances on their side often times does not attain the success they desire. It greatly impresses me that some of the countries with the richest natural resources on the earth, such as the Latin American countries live with such poverty.

What determines the future of a country, a city, or a person? Spiritual forces determine those results—forces that do not obey barriers of space or time. They are called blessings or curses.[27]

LANGUAGE OF THE KINGDOMS

Even if I already mentioned this subject briefly, I think it is necessary to consider it again. Each kingdom has a language to express itself. The language of the kingdom of God is intercession. The language of the kingdom of darkness is accusation. Hebrews 7:25 shows us that even today, our Lord Jesus Christ is interceding intercession. "Hence, also, He is able to save forever those who draw near to God through Him, since He always lives to make intercession for them."

Now, it is painful to see how such a great truth is neglected so. As I see it, there are few things that God looks for. One of them, of course, is when He seeks worshipers in spirit and in truth. Another one is when He says, "And I searched for a man among them who should build up the wall and stand in the gap before Me for the land, that I should not destroy it; but I found no one" (Ezekiel 22:30).

Intercession is the life of the Church. It is the language of the kingdom of God. It reflects the character and personality of

Christ. I am one who believes that every believer has been called by God to be an intercessor, and I disagree with the criterion that a special call or gift is needed to be an intercessor.

On the other hand, the kingdom of darkness also has its own language, which reflects the character of its king: accusation. The devil is the accuser of the brethren (see Revelation 12:10).

You will understand that when a believer is part of an accusation, he is aligning his conduct to the kingdom of darkness, contributing to the strengthening of that kingdom and bringing a curse upon himself.

The most common form of accusation is through gossiping and criticism, but sadly I have also sadly verified there are persons that pray "accusing prayers."

"He who turns away his ear from listening to the law, even his prayer is an abomination" (Proverbs 28:9).

"*And you were dead in your trespasses and sins,* in which you formerly walked according to the course of this world, according to the prince of the power of the air, of the spirit that is now working in the sons of disobedience. Among them we too all formerly lived in the lusts of our flesh, *indulging the desires of the flesh* and of the mind, and were by nature children of wrath, even as the rest" (Ephesians 2:1–3).

"These are grumblers, finding fault, *following after their own lusts;* they speak arrogantly, flattering people for the sake of gaining an advantage. But you, beloved, ought to remember the words that were spoken beforehand by the apostles of our Lord Jesus Christ, that they were saying to you, "'In the last time there shall be mockers, *following after their own ungodly lusts.* These are the ones who cause divisions, worldly-minded, devoid of the Spirit'" (Jude 1:16–19).

When the Word speaks of "sensual," it refers to the action of the soul. I have named those who are guided and react according to their senses and their emotions and not by thier spirit: "soulish people."

There is a very special connection between the tongue and the soul. Surely, because speech is the manifestation of decision.

"And the tongue is a fire, the very world of iniquity; the tongue is set among our members as that *which defiles the entire body*, and sets on fire the course of our life, and is set on fire by hell" (James 3:6).

"*For where jealousy and selfish ambition exist, there is disorder and every evil thing*" (James 3:16–17).

"Therefore thus says the LORD: "If you return, I will restore you, and you shall stand before me. If you utter what is precious, and not what is worthless, *you shall be as my mouth.* They shall turn to you, but you shall not turn to them" (Jeremiah 15:19, RSV).

"Then your light will break out like the dawn, and your recovery will speedily spring forth; and your righteousness will go before you; the glory of the Lord will be your rear guard. Then you will call, and the Lord will answer; you will cry, and He will say, 'Here I am.' *If you remove the yoke from your midst, the pointing of the finger, and speaking wickedness*" (Isaiah 58:8–9).

What we need, then, is to amend the way we speak by abstaining from accusation; learning to intercede, and by learning to abide in the language of the kingdom of God.

The devil does not need to do much if the believers are helping him by accusing and attacking one another. Now we have reached the root of the problem. There are many interested in learning the strategies of war, spiritual mapping, etc. Before that, however, it is necessary to cleanse ourselves because the entire problem started because we did not align ourselves to the will of God in the first place.

I am sorry to say that I have seen, over and over again, painful casualties because these concepts have been overlooked.

I conclude this section with these extraordinary and revealing scriptures:

"I call heaven and earth to witness against you today, that I have set before you life and death, the blessing and the curse. So choose life in order that you may live, you and your descendants" (Deuteronomy 30:19).

All our decisions have consequences.

"Now it shall be, if you will diligently obey the Lord your God, being careful to do all His commandments which I command you today, the Lord your God will set you high above all the nations of the earth *and all these blessings shall come upon you and overtake you, if you will obey the Lord your God*" (Deuteronomy 28:1–2).

"But it shall come about, *if you will not obey the Lord your God, to observe to do all His commandments and His statutes with which I charge you today, that all these curses shall come upon you and overtake you*" (Deuteronomy 28:15).

It is important to state that our interaction with the kingdoms will have an effect that will overflow into our own lives. The blessings and curses run through the generational lineage and affect our descendants (see Deuteronomy 7:9 and Exodus 34:6–7). As a matter of fact, we ourselves are fruit of the interaction of our ancestors with the kingdoms.

"Please inquire of *past generations,* and consider the things searched out by their fathers. *For we are only of yesterday and know nothing,* because our days on earth are as a shadow. Will they not teach you and tell you, and bring forth words from their minds?" (Job 8:8–10).

PART TWO

How Spiritual Warfare Is Carried Out

After sharing the theoretical elements of spiritual warfare in the previous section, I wish to take you to the practical steps to move against the enemy. Do not forget that during this study, we have taken the perspective of a local church, so you will surely find the advice that is directly geared to my colleagues, the pastors. Nevertheless, the fact that you are not a full-time minister does not mean that you cannot find your place among the group of people who need each other for this important initiative.

THE TOTAL DIAGRAM

Once and again, in many countries, I have found believers who approach me and share an authentic burden for their church, city, or nation and ask, "What should we do? Where do we begin?"

I asked the Lord to provide a simple answer, very graphic and easy to understand. I will not forget the inspiration of the Holy Spirit during a seminar in the beautiful city of Kuala Lumpur. The result is the diagram we are going to discuss next *(Figure 5.1)*.

The diagram refers to spiritual warfare, taking into consideration the way God describes the division of the human being in spirit, soul, and body.[28] I am persuaded that to be successful in spiritual warfare and to see the difference once it has taken place, we need a coordinated strategy in the three areas God gave man. (figure 5.1)

"Now may the God of peace Himself sanctify *you entirely;* and may *your spirit and soul and body* be preserved complete, without blame at the coming of our Lord Jesus Christ" (1 Thessalonians 5:23).

"Then the Lord God formed man of dust from the ground, and breathed into his nostrils the breath of life; and man became a living being" (Genesis 2:7), or as it reads in the King James Version, "and man became a living soul."

"For the word of God is living and powerful, and sharper than any two-edged sword, piercing even to the division of *soul and spirit, and of joints and marrow,* and is a discerner of the thoughts and intents of the heart" (Hebrews 4:12, NKJV).

The three parts of the human being work closely knitted and joined together. The action of one of them undoubtedly influences the other ones.

In the case of a believer, the human spirit exercises influence upon the soul and the body. (See Romans 8:14 and Proverbs 18:14.) In a given moment, a decision of the soul can make a person fall into sin and affect his spirit and soul. Or, a situation that interests exclusively the area of the flesh, for example, an anesthesia or an accident or trauma, can become a door for demonization that will affect the emotional and spiritual well-being of a person.

On the other hand, we want to launch ourselves into answering particular problems that hinder evangelism. Let us study how to diagnose the spiritual situation over a determined territory, the treatment that needs to be applied, and the expected results. I will also take the time to include evidence the Bible provides about the application of the principles of spiritual warfare in the ministry of Jesus Christ and the apostles.

	HUMAN AS A ...LE	THE CHALLENGE SPIRITUAL WARFARE	WHY THE INHERITANCE	THE DIAGNOSTIC	SPIRITUAL CARTOGRAPHY
T H E T O T A L S C H E M E	...SSALONIANS 5:23			T H E D I A G N O S T I C	
	SPIRIT	EPHESIANS 6:12, EPHESIANS 1:21, COLOSSIANS 2:15 Principalities, Powers, Rulers of the Darkness of This World, Spiritual Wickedness in High Places	SPIRITUAL INHERITANCE • Generations • National Sins • Family Spirits		SPIRITUAL FACTOR ROMANS 1:20
	SOUL	2 CORINTHIANS 10:3-5 Strongholds, Arguments, Pretensions, Thoughts, Structures, Ideas, Concepts, Ideologies, Idyosincrasy, Culture	ENVIRONMENTAL INHERITANCE • Personality • Idyosincrasy • Culture		HISTORIC OR SPIRITUAL FACTOR
	BODY	DEUTERONOMY 28:23, ISAIAH 25:7, JOB 37:19, 2 CORINTHIANS 4:4 Physical Consequences, Covering of Darkness, Veil of Blindness, Opposition to the Gospel	GENETIC INHERITANCE		PHYSICAL FACTOR PSALM 115

The left margin vertical letters: T H E T R E A T M E N T

THE WORK OF THE CHURCH		THE BATTLE	THE MINISTRY OF JESUS CHRIST	THE MINISTRY OF THE APOSTLES

WARFARE PRAYER
EPHESIANS 3:10
 	
PSALM 103:19-20
"BIND AND LOOSE"
MATTHEW 18:18
 	
INTERCESSION
 	
PROPHETIC
  INTERCESSION
 	
PROPHETIC ACTS
 	
SPIRITUAL
  MINISTRATION
ISAIAH 58:6
	W
	H
	A'
	T
	
	I
	T
		CLASH OF POWERS	PRAYER
			MINISTRY
			MARK 1:35
			
			AND EVEN
			TODAY:
			ACTS 7:25
				ACTS 6:4
				
				"But we will give ourselves continually to prayer..."

PREACHING OF
  THE GOSPEL
MARK 1:15
 	
THE DESTRUCTION
  OF "STRUCTURES"
JEREMIAH 1:10,
COLOSSIANS 2:20,
GALATIANS 4:1-9
 	
HOPE
LUKE 4:16-18
	P
	R
	O
	D
		CLASH OF TRUTHS	MINISTRY OF
			PREACHING
			AND
			TEACHING
			
			MARK 1:14-15
			MARK 1:21-22
			MARK 1:38
			LUKE 4:16-18
				"And to the ministry of the word."

PROPHETIC ACTS
 	
MINISTRY
ISAIAH 58:7
 	
CHURCH
  ORGANIZATION
  FOR EVANGELISM
EPHESIANS 4:11-13
	U
	C
	E
	S
		CLASH OF LOYALTIES	MINISTRY OF
			HEALING,
			Deliverance
			MARK 1:23-31
			MARK 1:32-34
			ISAIAH 58:6-7
				"And the number of the disciples multiplied greatly"

(Figure 5.1)

6

The Challenge

*Then comes the end, when He delivers up the kingdom to
the God and Father, when He has abolished all rule and all
authority and power.*

*For He must reign until He has put all His enemies
under His feet.*

1 Corinthians 15:24–25

Just as we have verified in the first section, there is no neutral
zone in this battle. Man finds himself involved in this cosmic
conflict called spiritual warfare. In it, as in all wars, there are enemies. The basic characteristic of these enemies, and probably the
reason why all the needed attention is not given to them, is their
invisibility. In this second section, we will continually refer to the
illustrative diagram (Figure 6.1) whose objective is to facilitate the
comprehension and eventual teaching of the subject. Please, feel
free to photocopy it or reproduce it in any way you see beneficial.
In the first part of the diagram—I have called this *the challenge*—
we will examine our invisible enemies, the forces that defy man in
his search for the blessing, may it be the evangelization of the
world or the transformation of our communities for the good of
their inhabitants.

THE HUMAN BEING AS A WHOLE	THE CHALLENGE: SPIRITUAL WARFARE
1 THESSALONIANS 5:23	
SPIRIT	EPHESIANS 6:12, EPHESIANS 1:21, COLOSSIANS 1:16, COLOSSIANS 2:15 **Principalities, Powers, Rulers of the Darkness of this World, Spiritual Wickedness in High Places, Authorities, Lordships, Names, Thrones, and Dominions (Hypsoma)**
SOUL	2 CORINTHIANS 10:3–5 **Strongholds, Arguments, Imaginations, Pretensions, Thoughts, Structures, Ideas, Concepts, Ideologies, Idyosincrasy, Culture**
BODY	DEUTERONOMY 28:23, ISAIAH 25:7, JOB 37:19, 2 CORINTHIANS 4:4 **Physical Consequences, Covering of Darkness, Veil of Blindness, Closed Door, Iron Bolt, Opposition to the Gospel**

(Figure 6.1)

According to our classification of spirit, soul, and body, we will group these enemies according to their own nature.

THE POWERS

In the Bible, there are four basic scriptures that list a group of spiritual beings, entities without a body that challenge men in the purely spiritual plane. Normally, believers refer to these spiritual beings by the name of demons, and it is commonly accepted to recognize that there are different demons of various ranges. For clarity reasons, we will group this set of spiritual beings under one category that we will call *The Powers*.

Ephesians 6:12, NIV, "For we do not wrestle against flesh and blood, but against *principalities*, against *powers*, against the *rulers of the darkness of this age*, against *spiritual hosts of wickedness in the heavenly places.*"

Ephesians 1:21, NIV, "Far above *all principality and power and might and dominion*, and *every name that is named*, not only in this age but also in that which is to come."

Colossians 1:16, NIV, "For by Him all things were created that are in heaven and that are on earth, visible and invisible, whether *thrones or dominions or principalities or powers*. All things were created through Him and for Him."

Colossians 2:15, NIV, "Having disarmed *principalities and powers*, He made a public spectacle of them, triumphing over them in it."

From these passages, we obtain a list that we will quote next, trying not to be repetitive and following the criteria established primarily by the New King James Version.

Principalities
Powers

Rulers of the darkness of this age
Spiritual hosts of wickedness in the heavenly places
Might
Dominion
Every name that is named, not only in this age but also in
        that which is to come
Thrones

It is evident that the kingdom of darkness has a hierarchy, in which the higher ranks rule or execute authority over the inferior ones.

Much has been said about each of these powers. I do not believe that it is necessary to proceed and describe each one of them. There is a large volume of bibliography at everyone's reach. Nevertheless, I would like to make a few observations. One of them refers to the fact that there seem to be three distinct groups in the biblical listing of the powers. One group conforms primarily to its basic characteristic: demons. Here we find the rulers of darkness and the spiritual hosts of wickedness. The second group corresponds more likely to the concepts of authority and power, and it clusters the principalities, powers, authorities, rulers, dominions, and thrones. And thirdly, we find a very special concept. It is the *names.* It is evident in the Bible that names hold a very important place, because their meaning causes an effect in the spiritual world. The example given to us by the book of Genesis, when God changes the patriarch Abram's name to Abraham, is very illustrative. What had not happened in twenty-four years since the promise had been given by God, happened in only one year after the name change. It is well-known that in the Old Testament the names of the sons, and even the places, were not chosen by chance or by fashion, but rather by their meaning—which would affect the life of the one who bore it. Even today, it is amazing to discover that the characteristics of a person correspond to the meaning of their name.

TERRITORIALITY OF THE SPIRITS

Today, the concept of *territoriality of the spirits* is widely recognized.[29] There was a time in which we gave ourselves to the task of studying the Word to be able to teach the concept of territoriality, which, mainly because of our Western mentality, was not only unknown but widely rejected, especially due to its intimate relationship with the concept of the *strong man*. However, biblical evidence and practical experience demonstrate that it is a biblical concept of utmost importance.

We have a very beautiful example in the fifth chapter of the gospel of Mark, about a man that was demonized and belonged to the country of the Gadarenes. Jesus comes to this place and has an encounter, a clash of power, with the unclean spirit that oppressed this man. Evidently, this demon, called Legion (which in this case expresses "a great multitude"), exercised an authority that surpassed that of the individual. It did not only demonize that particular man, but it went much further. It was exactly what we call today a territorial spirit, a demon that has territorial or geographical authority. Where do I get support for such a statement? Let us go on with the biblical narration. Jesus came to the country of the Gadarenes and as soon as He came, there met Him, out of the tombs, a man with an unclean spirit. When he saw Jesus, he cried out with a loud voice. Answering to a question from the Lord, the spirit replies, "'My name is Legion; for we are many.' And he begged him eagerly not to send them out of the country." In the English version, the reading "not to send them out of the country"[30] makes it very clear. It is evident that the unclean spirit wanted to stay in that area or territory because it enjoyed a privilege it would not have in another place. This is what we understand as territorial authority. The President of my country has authority in Guatemala, but even if he is respected and appreciated in another nation, he simply lacks the same privileges there.

When Jesus gave them permission, the unclean spirits came out of the man, and entered a herd of swine numbering about two thousand. What happened next is very revealing. This man obviously feels love and gratitude towards Jesus—which is natural since the Lord just made him free. The Gadarene wants to follow Jesus, but something very interesting happens. The Lord Jesus Christ refuses, and tells him, "Go home to your friends, and tell them how much the Lord has done for you, and how He has had mercy on you."

It impresses me to see that this man, having been demonized by a legion of demons a moment before, was immediately entrusted with the ministry of evangelism after being set free by Jesus. The result of the liberation is even more impressive. The Gadarene goes and preaches the gospel in Decapolis, which as you may know, means "ten cities." By this we understand that the oppression manifested through this man is changed into liberty to go and bring the gospel to ten cities. The power that this unclean spirit had exercised over Decapolis had been broken.

This truth takes us to the concept of the *strong man*, a very particular phrase that appears in the gospels of Matthew and Luke, within a context of teaching about demonology. It is our Lord Jesus Christ who explains the need to confront the *strong man*, to bind him and overpower him in order to plunder his goods.

"When a strong man, fully armed, guards his own homestead,

his possessions are undisturbed; but when someone stronger than he attacks him and overpowers him, he takes away from him all his armor on which he had relied, and distributes his plunder" (Luke 11:21–22).

"Or how can anyone enter the strong man's house and carry off his property, unless he first binds the strong man? And then he will plunder his house" (Matthew 12:29).

To me, it is obvious that if the Lord wanted to say strong spirit, He would have done so. But He said strong man. This contains good teaching for us. Many times there is a strong man; literally, a human being who has made a covenant with the devil or with certain demons, and who has been given spiritual dominion over a determined territory. The understanding of this concept can be clarified if we use a simile. When a minister of the gospel, a servant of God, is greatly used by the Lord, we usually use the expression "He is anointed." What does this mean? It means that this brother has a relationship with the Lord—Who has anointed him with the Holy Spirit and power. It is generally accepted that this is due to an intimate communion with God, through worship, prayer, fasting, and the Word of the Lord, that is to say, lines of communication or communion that this particular minister constantly keeps with God. In the same way, there are persons who dedicate themselves to weaving lines of communication with the devil. Usually we call them warlocks or sorcerers. It is men or women who, in order to obtain power, praise, and worship establish covenants with Satan. The result is what we find in the Bible as a *strong man,* a person who is "connected" to Satan, who serves him, and through whom the devil exercises authority or power over a territory, community, or a social conglomerate. On the other hand, it is evident that the devil, knowing his limitations, strives to use a physical element to serve his purposes. The

Scriptures teach us that demons seek a human body in which to live (Matthew 12:43 and Luke 11:24). They even resign themselves to using animal bodies (Mark 5:12).

Our interest in this subject derives from the fact that we have seen over and over again that when the strong man is vanquished in a given territory, the inhabitants become free to receive the light of the gospel.[31] The testimony of what God has done through the prayers of His children in Guatemala, and the conquering of Maximon in the city called Almolonga, "the Miracle City," is already legendary.[32]

As an affirmation about the subject of territoriality of the spirits, I recommend that the reader carefully study the two following scriptures and their context. I am sure that as you do it, you will obtain great blessing.

The Second Book of Kings 17:24–28, RSV, reads, "And the king of Assyria brought people from Babylon, Cuthah, Avva, Hamath, and Sepharvaim, and placed them in the cities of Samaria instead of the people of Israel; and they took possession of Samaria, and dwelt in its cities. And at the beginning of their dwelling there, they did not fear the LORD; therefore the LORD sent lions among them, which killed some of them. So the king of Assyria was told, 'The nations which you have carried away and placed in the cities of Samaria do not know the law of the God of the land; therefore He has sent lions among them, and behold, they are killing them, because they do not know the *law of the God of the land.*' Then the king of Assyria commanded, 'Send there one of the priests whom you carried away thence; and let him go and dwell there, and teach them *the law of the God of the land.*' So one of the priests whom they had carried away from Samaria came and dwelt in Bethel, and taught them how they should fear the LORD."

Daniel 10:12–14 reads, "Then he said to me, 'Do not be afraid, Daniel, for from the first day that you set your heart on understanding this and on humbling yourself before your God, your words were heard, and I have come in response to your words. But the prince of the kingdom of Persia was withstanding me for twenty-one days; then behold, Michael, one of the chief princes, came to help me, for I had been left there with the kings of Persia. Now I have come to give you an understanding of what will happen to your people in the latter days, for the vision pertains to the days yet future.'"

Daniel 10:20–21 reads, "Then he said, 'Do you understand why I came to you? But I shall now return to fight against the *prince of Persia;* so I am going forth, and behold, *the prince of Greece* is about to come. However, I will tell you what is inscribed in the writing of truth. Yet there is no one who stands firmly with me against these forces except Michael *your prince.*'"

THE STRUCTURES

In second place, we have a series of words that the Bible gives us that have their location in their corresponding area of the soul as a common denominator. It is what we will call "the structures." The Scripture *par excellence* is 2 Corinthians 10:3–5, NKJV, "For though we walk in the flesh, we do not war according to the flesh. For the weapons of our warfare are not carnal but mighty in God for pulling down *strongholds,* casting down *arguments* [imaginations, ASV] and *every high thing* [lofty thing, NASB; proud obstacle, RSV; pretension, NIV], that exalts itself against the knowledge of God, bringing every *thought* into captivity to the obedience of Christ."

From the above verse and the natural evolution of these concepts we find a more detailed list that follows:

Strongholds

Arguments

Imaginations

Every high thing that exalts itself against the knowledge of God

Thoughts

Ideas

Ideologies

Concepts

Structures

Idiosyncrasy

Culture

As you have seen, each word listed above defines elements that make up the way human beings think and express. They are the basic structures with which man expresses what he feels, believes, and wishes. Those, then, are elements that belong to the area of the human soul. They refer to the expression of the intellect or mind, the emotions or feelings, and the will or volitional capacity. Given that those are blocks that constitute the expression of the human soul, I have decided to call them structures, because I realize that each one constitutes a block upon which the next one is built. In that way, adhering to the biblical language, the basic element is a thought, and the final structure, completely developed, would be a stronghold.

If we list these words in a progressive development sequence, you will see how the concepts evolve.

A thought is the basic element. The Bible tells us that each one of us has to bring every thought captive to the obedience of Christ (2 Corinthians 10:5).

Here, I want to share an illustration that can greatly bless you. While visiting an egg-packing and distributing plant, I had a very special experience. I saw a conveyor belt that carried the eggs to be checked before being packed. There were operators at both sides of the belt who would choose the eggs and place them in their corresponding boxes. Under the belt, a strong light was installed. The light went through the belt, illuminating the inside of the eggs. In this way, the operators could make sure the eggs were all right. At the same time, they could see if any of them were spoiled. If that were the case, they would immediately set it apart and throw it in the garbage. While I observed the process, God spoke to my heart and made real to me the need to bring every thought captive to the obedience of Christ. It is necessary that we judge every thought that comes to our minds and expose it to the light of the Word of God. Only the Word will indicate to us if that thought is edifying for us and takes us to the glorious freedom in Christ.

"For the word of God is living and active and sharper than any two-edged sword, and piercing as far as the division of soul and spirit, of both joints and marrow, and able to *judge the thoughts* and intentions of the heart" (Hebrews 4:12).

A man is composed of what he believes (Proverbs 23:7)[33], so the quality of thoughts we allow to enter into our system will have a positive or negative effect in our life. The thoughts we let into our mind will affect everything that we do. That is why the Word says "not to think beyond what is written" (1 Corinthians 4:6, NKJV). I will share a more recent example of what happened to me, to ratify the teaching I gave before. Formerly, I used an Apple® computer that had a very interesting system. I used to move my documents from a laptop to my home computer, inserting a disk. When the disk was inserted the computer sent me a message to wait, indicating that the machine was checking the disk for viruses that would harm my computer. That is what God commands us to do. We should examine every thought, comparing it to the Word of God—so that we do not think beyond what is written and concentrate on thinking only what He has approved.

"And the peace of God, which surpasses all comprehension, shall guard your hearts and your minds in Christ Jesus. Finally, brethren, *whatever is true, whatever is honorable, whatever is right, whatever is pure, whatever is lovely, whatever is of good repute, if there is any excellence and anything worthy of praise, let your mind dwell on these things*" (Philippians 4:7–8).

The conclusion is that each one of us should be careful with the thoughts that enter our system. We should bring *every* thought into captivity to the obedience of Christ. If we do not do it, we are at risk of letting one of the thoughts that have not been taken captive become an argument that exalts itself against the knowledge of God, that is, a thought contrary to the Word of God.

Now, if an argument or a high thing that exalts itself against the knowledge of God penetrates the barriers of our mind (soul), we can be at the doors of creating a stronghold that will eventually enslave us.

Continuing with the sequence of progressive development, a series of *thoughts* or high things become an *idea*. A series of ideas gives way to a *concept*. A series of concepts becomes an *argument*. Several arguments combined form what we call a *stronghold*.

We have to remember that a stronghold has the connotation of being a prison designed not to allow the ones inside to come out. Or also, a stronghold can be a castle designed so that the ones that are outside cannot come in. In either way, it is something that becomes an obstacle, an impediment of total freedom.

A series of ideas or strongholds constitute an *ideology* that can, in a given moment, enslave many people, as has been the case of communism or nazism.

The ideas, ideologies and concepts that join together a conglomerate of people—be it territorial in the case of a nation, or of a particular race—give place to what we call the *idiosyncrasy* that is typical of the place or the *culture* of a people, understanding that these are their set of beliefs, concepts, ideas, artistic expression, religious expression, etc.

IMAGINATIONS (*LOGISMOS*) AND HIGH THINGS (*HUPSOMA*)

"Casting down arguments and every high thing that exalts itself against the knowledge of God, bringing every thought into captivity to the obedience of Christ" (2 Corinthians 10:5).

Dr. C. Peter Wagner has been a friend and mentor to me. On one occasion, when I finished my exposition, he told me, "Harold, you are not my student, but you are like a son to me, so I want to share something with you." He told me what he had investigated about the great difference between arguments and high things. As a matter of fact, the difference is so important that technically we should place the arguments in the area of the soul and the high things in the area of the spirit. I decided to leave the diagram as it was because it is easier to understand (and to teach). Nevertheless, I thought it necessary to include this explanation.

Arguments, thoughts, and concepts belong to the group of the Greek word *logismos* and share a human origin, as do thoughts, decisions and human actions. As we saw in detail in the first section of this book, what men decide and do has an effect or consequence in the spiritual world. This word *logismos* belongs totally to the areas of the soul: mind, intellect, feelings, emotions and will.

On the contrary, the "high thing that exalts itself against the knowledge of God" has a spiritual origin. J. Blunck, quoted by

Dr. Wagner[34], says, "The New Testament use of *hypsoma* probably reflects astrological ideas, and hence denotes cosmic powers." The Scriptures in Romans 8:39 and 2 Corinthians 10:5 refer to powers directed against God that seek to intervene between God and man. They are possibly related to the *stoicheion kosmos,* the rudiments of the world (Colossians 2:8, 20). Even if these seem so high and powerful, that we have to resist them energetically and vigorously (2 Corinthians 10:5), knowing that not even they can separate believers from Christ (Romans 8:39).

The high things are the result of cosmic powers translated into astrological ideas designed to separate man from the true God. Probably one of the best examples that exist in this sense is related to the zodiac and the horoscope. How many people let spirits enter their lives through an apparently harmless way that is nothing more than the product of the spirit of divination? It seems incredible to us that there are people totally dominated by the horoscope—to the point of not acting. Some do not even leave their homes without consulting it. The truth is that they are not dominated by ideas, but by the cosmic powers behind those ideas.

It is good to recognize when it is an argument and when it is a high thing, and their differences, but what is especially important is to know that the name of Jesus is more than enough to bind and conquer both.

HOW THE POWERS MANIFEST

As established before, demons or "powers" are disembodied spirits. How is it possible then that beings without a body affect men—and even territories—that are physical? The inclusion of an intermediate element between the powers and man becomes necessary. Secular mentality places man as a being composed of body and soul. However, the Bible speaks of three: spirit, soul and body (1 Thessalonians 5:23). The intermediate element between the spirit and the body is the soul. As we know, the soul consists of three parts: the mind, the emotions, and the will. It is in this area that ideas, feelings, and decisions are found. As we established in the first section, in chapter four, the devil does not have power in him, but it becomes necessary for him to use the only additional source of power that exists in the universe, which proceeds from the soul of man. Thus, it is not strange that the powers use what we call structures to enslave men. Within the concept of structures, we have to include ideologies, culture, and idiosyncrasies, but of course the key word is *strongholds. The powers influence the minds of men to create strongholds,* ways of thinking that are contrary to the Word of God, to separate men from the divine plan, and in doing so, reduces them to slavery.

THE EFFECTS IN THE NATURAL WORLD

The powers act through mental structures, producing physical consequences on people and even upon their territory. Man finds himself in a hostile environment to him (1 John 5:19 and John 17:15). His confrontation against the world, the devil, and the flesh is continuous (Ephesians 2:1–3). "But each one is tempted when he is carried away and enticed by his own lust. Then when lust has conceived, it gives birth to sin; and when sin is accomplished, it brings forth death" (James 1:14–15). In the same way that life is light (John 1:4), death is darkness. As I understand it, each sin—personal or corporate—constitutes a thread in the fabric of the covering of darkness. Romans 6:23 says, "For the wages of sin is death, but the free gift of God is eternal life in Christ Jesus our Lord." This is how the covering of darkness is woven over a city or a nation, because of the sins of its inhabitants. Imagine the effect of sin generation after generation over a territory.[35]

Isaiah 25:7, NKJV "And He will destroy on this mountain the surface of *the covering* cast over all people, and the veil that is spread over all nations."

Second Corinthians 4:4 *"In whose case the god of this world has blinded the minds of the unbelieving, that they might not see the light of the gospel of the glory of Christ, who is the image of God."*

When there is a covering of darkness, one of the most impressive characteristics is the fact that the people under the covering are practically unaware of the existence of the problems. Even the believers themselves do not seem to discern the causes of the blindness while they are under it. When I arrive at the different nations where I have ministered, I have asked myself many times how is it possible that strongholds and their consequences which are very obvious to us as foreigners can be so hidden from the ones living there. I was impressed to find the biblical answer to this question.

Job 37:19, KJV "Teach us what we shall say unto him; for we cannot order our speech by reason of *darkness.*"

In a city or a social conglomerate where there is a covering of darkness, all the inhabitants are "under" that darkness. The darkness alters their way of perceiving reality. What we call the Western mentality, for example, makes man believe that the supernatural does not exist. The "Greek"[36] mentality denies the reality of the spiritual world because it cannot explain it through reason. That is why there are many believers in America and Europe who do not believe that demons exist. The power of the strongholds is such that I have found that in certain countries laws are promulgated in relation to the collective mental strongholds. In a certain country, I learned that the government regulates the amount of inheritance that can be given to a son. They limit it to a maximum amount while the government keeps the rest to take care of the person until the day he dies. They are convinced that 98% of all the inhabitants will die of Alzheimer's disease. You should have seen the surprise in their eyes when I commented that in my country we hardly have that disease. Immediately they thought of their food intake. I thought of their mental intake.

In another continent, I found that the concept of feminine menopause—so common in the American continent, to the point of being a must for all women, and, by the way, being a source of great profit to the pharmaceutical companies—was absolutely nonexistent.

Also, in another country, Congress found it necessary to prohibit the import of ultrasound medical equipment—so popular in other countries to see the fetus inside the mother's womb. By performing an ultrasound many families could corroborate that they had a baby girl and not a boy—as the social culture demands—and many couples decided to abort the baby. With the purpose of stopping the increase in the number of abortions, the government decided to prevent the entry of those machines to the country. This is a curious way of fighting against abortion. The covering of darkness produces fruits that are almost unbelievable. Even acts and customs that go against the Word of God are justified simply because they are part of the culture and the history of the society in that place.

The covering of darkness plays a key role in the hindrance of prayers, as is the case of the prophet Daniel. God's answer was immediate. However, it took twenty-one days for the angel Gabriel, bearer of the answer, to overcome the resistance of the prince of Persia and the covering of darkness. In this particular case, undoubtedly the sins of Persia, and the sins of the apostasy of Israel, had caused its captivity at the hands of Babylon and the subsequent captivity at the hands of Persia—sins of "their fathers" for which the prophet humiliated himself (Daniel 9 and 10).

The covering of darkness is decisive while evangelizing. Today, we all understand the concept of open heavens, knowing that is the way of having an effective evangelism.

"And He said to him, 'Truly, truly, I say to you, you shall see the heavens opened, and the angels of God ascending and descending on the Son of Man'" (John 1:51).

And, when the Word of God defines the role of the angels, it says, "Are they not all ministering spirits, sent out to render service for the sake of those who will inherit salvation?" (Hebrews 1:14).

Deuteronomy 28:23, "And the heaven which is over your head shall be bronze, and the earth which is under you, iron."

Following the sequence of our diagram, when we focus on the effects of the powers and the strongholds over people and territories, we have to point out the following extremes:

a. The covering of darkness represents a way of thinking marked by "the high things that exalt themselves against the knowledge of God." Maybe it is very easy to imagine a pagan country, absolutely given to idolatry. But what would you think of doing a little mental exercise by thinking what used to be said in communist Russia, "Religion is the opium of the masses," or the city of New York and Mammon, the god of riches? The culture of a country exactly reflects the invisible powers. It is easy to understand what type of covering prevails over France, if we think that they produce the best perfumes (smell), the best wines and foods (taste). They are the leaders in areas pertaining to the arts, architecture, esthetics, and others (sight). Not to mention that they excel in sculpture, fashion, fabric, furs and more (touch). Even their language itself is pleasing to the hearer (ear). The marked hedonism of the culture reveals the spirit of sensuality that has been produced by that covering of darkness.

b. Through the thought patterns of a people, their actions are molded. Through these, certain spirits are lifted on a throne, that is to say, a position of dominion or might.[37]

c. The covering of darkness, plagued with pride obstacles, brings forth a veil of blindness over the people who are under it (2 Corinthians 4:4), to obstruct evangelism.

d. Closed doors, bars of iron (Revelation 3:7).

e. Lastly, it is necessary to mention that as a consequence of the powers and strongholds, even the natural elements of a territory are affected. I do not only refer to social conditions of corruption, poverty, lack of productivity, bondage because of vices and illness, but even the natural conditions of the territory.

In the particular case of Almolonga, in Guatemala, the population had been held captive by poverty, alcoholism, domestic violence, witchcraft, and idolatry. Added to this was the natural factor of the aridness of the land, the lack of water and the subsequent lack of productivity of the land. It is interesting to note that the land was covered by large amounts of stones, of all sizes. The transformation that Almolonga has undergone through spiritual warfare and evangelism—which has caused that today 90% of its inhabitants are born-again believers—has resulted in a profound social impact that has caused extraordinary blessings. The transformation has also resulted in the fact that the last jail closed its doors seven years ago due to the lack of prisoners. This might seem marvelous, but it is equally important to see that God has literally healed the land (2 Chronicles 7:14) and it has become the most fertile valley in the country. Here, water springs up from the ground and the most marvelous vegetables you can imagine are produced in abundant crops that defy one's imagination.

When I hear the exclamations of surprise because of this testimony, I think that the amazement that sometimes is caused by what God does is amusing because He is only confirming His Word.

"Now it shall be, if you will diligently obey the Lord your God, being careful to do all His commandments which I command you today, the Lord your God will set you high above all the nations of the earth.

And all these blessings shall come upon you and overtake you, if you will obey the Lord your God.

Blessed shall you be in the city, and blessed shall you be in the country.

Blessed shall be the offspring of your body and the produce of your ground and the offspring of your beasts, the increase of your herd and the young of your flock.

Blessed shall be your basket and your kneading bowl.

The Lord will command the blessing upon you in your barns and in all that you put your hand to, and He will bless you in the land which the Lord your God gives you.

And the Lord will make you abound in prosperity, in the offspring of your body and in the offspring of your beast and in the produce of your ground, in the land which the Lord swore to your fathers to give you.

The Lord will open for you His good storehouse, the heavens, to give rain to your land in its season and to bless all the work of your hand; and you shall lend to many nations, but you shall not borrow.

And the Lord shall make you the head and not the tail, and you only shall be above, and you shall not be underneath, if you will listen to the commandments of the Lord your God, which I charge you today, to observe them carefully [. . .]

and do not turn aside from any of the words which I command you today, to the right or to the left, to go after other gods to serve them.

But it shall come about, if you will not obey the Lord your God, to observe to do all His commandments and His statutes with which I charge you today, that all these curses shall come upon you and overtake you.

Cursed shall you be in the city, and cursed shall you be in the country.

Cursed shall be your basket and your kneading bowl.

Cursed shall be the offspring of your body and the produce of your ground, the increase of your herd and the young of your flock.

And the heaven which is over your head shall be bronze, and the earth which is under you, iron.

The Lord will make the rain of your land powder and dust; from heaven it shall come down on you until you are destroyed.

So all these curses shall come on you and pursue you and overtake you until you are destroyed, because you would not obey the Lord your God by keeping His commandments and His statutes which He commanded you."

DEUTERONOMY 28:1–5, 8, 11–18, 23, 24, and 45

The Scripture explains well that creation itself is waiting for the Church to do its part of the plan of God, working towards the redemption of each of our nations.

"For the anxious longing of the creation waits eagerly for the revealing of the sons of God. For the creation was subjected to futility, not of its own will, but because of Him who subjected it, in hope that *the creation itself also will be set free from its slavery to corruption into the freedom of the glory of the children of God.* For we know that the whole creation groans and suffers the pains of childbirth together until now. And not only this, but also we ourselves, having the first fruits of the Spirit, even we ourselves groan within ourselves, waiting eagerly for our adoption as sons, the redemption of our body" (Romans 8:19–23).

7

The Reason for
the Problems

Who has performed and accomplished it, calling forth the
generations from the beginning? "I, the Lord, am the first;
and with the last I am He."

ISAIAH 41:4

THE GENERATIONAL CONCEPT

Everything has a reason for being. As the Word says, "Like a sparrow in its flitting, like a swallow in its flying, so a curse without cause does not alight" (Proverbs 26:2). To understand the reasons that have brought our societies to be what they are today, it is necessary to understand a concept that is greatly ingrained in the heart of God and in the Word. It is the concept of "generations"; a word that we find more than 700 times in the Bible.

Modern-day people usually think only about "their" life. That is to say, they think of their 60, 70 or 80-year life span. This is a very great mistake, because in biblical terms the life of a person is not limited to the years he lives on this earth. God sees much further than us. When God sees a person, He can see from his ancestors to his descendants.

I like to think of man as a tree. It is true it has branches, leaves and fruit we see in the tree, but in no way can we be deceived into thinking that this is all there is. We all know that the tree would not exist without a structure to nourish and sustain it, called the root. We cannot see it, it is under the ground, but we know it is there and the tree originated from it. In the same manner, the man we now see is the fruit of past generations.

When God explains why Abraham was to become a great and strong nation, and why all nations would be blessed in him, He makes it clear that Abraham had assimilated the important concept of the generations: "For I know him, *that he will command his children and his household after him,* and they shall keep the way of the LORD to do justice and judgment, that the LORD may bring upon Abraham that which He hath spoken of him" (Genesis 18:18–19).

God is a generational God. Over and over again, He introduces Himself as the God of Abraham, Isaac and Jacob (Exodus 3:6).

Maybe we do not pay much attention to this concept, but undoubtedly it is a very important fact for the Lord.

In Hebrews, God says, "And, so to speak, through Abraham even Levi, who received tithes, paid tithes, *for he was still in the loins of his father when Melchizedek met him*" (Hebrews 7:9–10).

Exodus 34 has always seemed exciting to me, where the Word says that God himself gave Moses the description of His name, "And the Lord descended in the cloud and stood there with him as he called upon the name of the Lord. Then the Lord passed by in front of him and proclaimed, 'The Lord, the Lord God, compassionate and gracious, slow to anger, and abounding in lovingkindness and truth; who keeps lovingkindness for thousands, who forgives iniquity, transgression and sin; yet He will by no means leave the guilty unpunished, visiting the iniquity of fathers on the children and on the grandchildren to the third and fourth generations'" (Exodus 34:5–7). I am impressed that among the basic elements of the character of God there is a reference to generations. I am fully persuaded that we serve a generational God.

"Know therefore that the Lord your God, He is God, the faithful God, who keeps His covenant and His lovingkindness *to a thousandth generation* with those who love Him and keep His commandments" (Deuteronomy 7:9).

"*He has remembered His covenant forever,* the word which He commanded *to a thousand generations,* the covenant which He made with *Abraham,* And His oath to *Isaac.* Then He confirmed it to *Jacob* for a statute, *to Israel as an everlasting covenant*" (Psalms 105:8–10).

INHERITANCE

Webster Dictionary defines the word inheritance in the following way:

1 a: the act of inheriting property b: the reception of genetic qualities by transmission from parent to offspring c: the acquisition of a possession, condition, or trait from past generations.
2: something that is or may be inherited.
3 a: tradition b: a valuable possession that is a common heritage from nature.
4 *obsolete:* possession.

According to that definition, we can inherit tangible things and also things that fall in the classification of intangible.

GENETIC INHERITANCE

We have all found ourselves before a newborn baby, making comments like "she has the eyes of her father" or "the smile of her mother." "He is as intelligent as his father" or "has the artistic abilities of his mother." These are common expressions. I think that the subject of genetic inheritance is clear to all. It refers to the physical characteristics and traits that we inherit from our parents. Furthermore, there is absolute consciousness that what is inherited can be something bad, not only good. It is like an insurance salesman who asks if there is diabetes or another inherited sickness in the family. The genetic inheritance is called that because it is transmitted in the genes. We can classify it in the area that concerns the body or the physical.

ENVIRONMENTAL INHERITANCE

Later, the scientists opened our eyes to the fact that not only physical traits are inherited. We also receive other things from our parents, invisible, intangible, but real, like the psychological characteristics—like personality and temperament—cultural characteristics—like language, our world view and our way to cope with reality—and, of course, the social conditions we received from our ancestors. This is called environmental inheritance because it is a product of the environment in which we grow and mature. We inherit factors that will influence our individual development, and we pass them on to our children in the same way.

If we take this concept and we translate it to a social conglomerate, we no longer talk of individuals but of cities and/or nations. Then we refer to the social consciousness or the personality of the city, the idiosyncrasy, and the culture.

A city is only a group of people. If people have a personality and a culture, we can understand that a city has its own personality and culture.

SPIRITUAL INHERITANCE

I have found many books and articles about genetic inheritance and even about environmental inheritance. However, I have not found much information about the subject of spiritual inheritance—which is strange because the Bible is full of references about this. In the same way we inherit physical and psychological factors, we also receive a spiritual inheritance. We would do well if we do not ignore this fact.

There is a scripture in the book of Job that not only helps us see the truth of what I have mentioned but also greatly impresses me:

> "Please inquire of past generations, and consider the things searched out by their fathers. *For we are only of yesterday and know nothing, because our days on earth are as a shadow. Will they not teach you and tell you, and bring forth words from their minds?*" Job 8:8–10

It is evident that the Word is speaking of what I call *the roots of men;* that is, that which exists even if we cannot see it.

> "*Behold, everyone who quotes proverbs will quote this proverb concerning you, saying, 'Like mother, like daughter. You are the daughter of your mother, who loathed her husband and children. You are also the sister of your sisters, who loathed their husbands and children. Your mother was a Hittite and your father an Amorite.*" Ezekiel 16:44–45

Over and over, God expresses the concept of spiritual inheritance. He says, "You shall not worship them or serve them; for I, the Lord your God, am a jealous God, *visiting the iniquity of the fathers on the children, on the third and the fourth generations* of those who hate Me" (Exodus 20:5).

I have conducted a study about the topic I call "The Lines of Iniquity" and how the sins of the fathers produce an iniquity, an inclination to the same kind of sin in their children. I have been able to clearly determine that if the cross of Calvary is not present, the children will inherit the spiritual weaknesses of their fathers.

There is a spiritual principle in the Bible that only a few people pay attention to: "*Each generation is destined to determine the integral future of the next generation.*" When I use the word integral, I refer to his whole being: spirit, soul and body (1 Thessalonians 5:23). All that we are and do will have a consequence or effect over our children.

"What do you mean by using this proverb concerning the land of Israel saying, '*The fathers eat the sour grapes, But the children's teeth are set on edge*'?" (Ezekiel 18:2).

INHERITANCE PROVIDES THE "REASON"
(Figure 7.1)

When we deal with the topic of spiritual warfare in a given city or nation, questions always arise concerning the reasons that took us to the point where we are now. How did this territorial spirit become a principality or power? Why did a covering of darkness develop? How? Why is there resistance to the Word?

The answers to these questions come when we analyze the inheritance which that city or nation has received. Just as a person becomes an extension of his parents, a whole generation in a city or nation is the extension of the generations that preceded it.

It is here that we have to mention ***national or corporate sins.***

THE HUMAN BEING AS A WHOLE	WHY THE INHERITANCE
1 THESSALONIANS 5:23 SPIRIT	**SPIRITUAL INHERITANCE** • Generations • National Sins • Familiar Spirits
SOUL	**FAMILY INHERITANCE** • Personality • Idyosincrasy • Culture
BODY	**GENETIC INHERITANCE**

(Figure 7.1)

These refer to sins committed by the community or by its representatives. It can be a collective sin, an action or omission for which all are responsible. Or else, it can be the sins of the ones who govern—*sins with consequences for all of society.*

When we speak of nations, we speak of *ethnos,* which means people, ethnicities, races. We had always thought that sin was something personal. However, it is not so. It is possible for an entire social conglomerate to sin, in many occasions in the name of "culture" or simply because no one has questioned if something that is a national habit is an abomination before the Lord. Such is the case of fairs, carnivals, processions, and pagan festivals. Educated, cultured citizens, in the full sense of the word, repeat these festivals over and over again without inquiring about the origin of these activities.

The second book of the prophet Samuel gives us a marvelous example of a sin with national consequences.

"Now there was a famine in the days of David for three years, year after year; and David sought the presence of the Lord. And the Lord said, 'It is for Saul and his bloody house, because he put the Gibeonites to death'" (2 Samuel 21:1).

The nation had suffered a famine for three years. King David decided to seek the Lord. (Oh, that we had rulers today who would seek the Lord when problems of national magnitude arise!) The reason for the problem that was whipping David's kingdom was not imputable to him or his generation. As a matter of fact, it was an inherited problem. It was Saul's fault—who by this time was already dead—but Israel and David, its king, suffered the consequences. The specific reason was the bloodshed of the Gibeonites.

We find this story in the book of Joshua. We will go back to it to understand what this verse refers to. When the inhabitants of

Gibeon heard what Joshua had done to Jericho and to Ai, they acted craftily and wearing worn-out clothes they posed as envoys (Joshua 9:3–5) "and Joshua made peace with them" (Joshua 9:15). Three days after they had made a covenant with them, the children of Israel realized they had been deceived but they could not kill them "because the leaders of the congregation had sworn to them by the Lord the God of Israel" (Joshua 9:18).

Nevertheless, many generations after that, Saul in his zeal for the children of Israel and Judah had broken the covenant that Joshua and the princes of Israel had made with the Gibeonites. Now, in the time of David—who had nothing to do with these actions—they were living the fulfillment of the law of sowing and reaping. Israel was receiving the consequences of corporate sin, a sin of national characteristics: the breaking of the covenant their fathers had made with the Gibeonites.

In this particular case, the sins of a ruler (Saul) had consequences that reached to all of the people in a future generation. The sin of the ruler opened a door for the devil to bring famine over the people, even though it was another generation with another ruler.

At this point it is fitting to mention *familiar spirits,* understanding these as the ones who adhere to a family and pass from generation to generation. There is an agreement about the fact that certain doors are opened to the evil one in a family and through those doors a familiar spirit finds a place. This spirit will give shape to a family until it reflects the characteristics of that particular spirit.

For the purpose of our subject, we can project the influence of these spirits to a social conglomerate. In such a way, it is said that in a city the great majority of the people share a common denominator in their behavior. For example, they can show an unusual level of a given characteristic, like violence or immorality, or are known for being a fearless people or lawless or other characteristics.

There is a popular consensus in my country that those who live in the east of the country are violent. In that area, there is a territorial spirit of violence that has gone from generation to generation over the families. It has come to the extent of shaping the character and personality of the inhabitants to the point of being nationally known for that characteristic.

What started as a generational familiar spirit has become a territorial power because the inhabitants have accepted that attitude and behavior in spite of it being contrary to the law of the Lord.

I conclude by saying that many of the circumstances in which we now live in the physical or soulical level, and even in the spiritual level, are the result of the acts and omissions of our ancestors. Both Nehemiah and David (in their respective books) instruct us about the need to seek forgiveness for the sins of our fathers. (See Nehemiah 1:4–7 and Daniel 9:3–19.)

8

The Diagnosis

Because that which is known about God is evident within them; for God made it evident to them.

For since the creation of the world His invisible attributes, His eternal power and divine nature, have been clearly seen, being understood through what has been made, so that they are without excuse.

ROMANS 1:19–20

One of the principles of what has been called "the art of war" is to know the enemy. (Figure 8.1)

Plans are established by counsel; by wise guidance wage war.

PROVERBS 20:18

Ecclesiastes 9:13–18 introduces a story whose conclusion is: "Wisdom is better than weapons of war."

If we want to be successful in spiritual warfare we have to be aware that we need precise knowledge about the battle conditions.

The Apostle Paul says, "I therefore so run, not as uncertainly; *so fight I, not as one that beateth the air*" (1 Corinthians 9:26).

THE HUMAN BEING AS A WHOLE		SPIRITUAL MAPPING
1 THESSALONIANS 5:23 **SPIRIT**	T H E	**SPIRITUAL FACTOR** ROMANS 1:20
SOUL	D I A G N O S T I C	**CULTURAL OR HISTORIC FACTOR**
BODY		**PHYSICAL FACTOR** PSALMS 115

(Figure 8.1)

SPIRITUAL MAPPING

I define spiritual mapping as a technique that provides us the equivalent to military espionage and intelligence. *Spiritual mapping is the way to discern, with precision, the powers in the spiritual kingdom, the structures in the cultural realm and its effects in the natural field.*

What an X-ray is to a physician, spiritual mapping is to an intercessor. The spiritual map obtained through spiritual mapping is the image taken of the heavenly places.

It does not mean that we are looking exclusively for demons but actually verifying which powers rule in a given territory.

The biblical principle based in Romans 1:18–20 is this: "The visible reveals the invisible to us. What we can see, explains what is hidden to our eyes."

Despite the abundance of bibliography in existence today, there are people who still doubt this discipline. Even though my task is not to convince them about this issue, I will draw their attention to the fact that for the ones on the side of darkness these concepts are no novelty whatsoever and the occultists do not lose their time questioning their validity.

I will only share three ideas that will surely draw the attention of the acute reader and prove to be an incentive to continue an investigation that could well be used by the Holy Spirit in your city or neighborhood.

1. The first reference comes from the book *Lucifer Dethroned* that literally says,

> There are two main magical areas in the highest ranks
> of the European frankmasonry. One is the search of the

supposed immortality through alchemy and tantric yoga. The other refers to the twin sciences of the megapolisomance and archeometry. Here are the definitions:

Megapolisomance: (*megapolis*, Greek term meaning a great city; *omanceI*, magic, like in necromancy, *crystalomancy*, [magic using crystal balls], chiromancy [palm reading, etc.]. Therefore, it refers to magic related to the construction of a city.

Archeometry, which means, "measures of ancient measurement." This is the magic science of what is also called "the proportionate measure of the earth." There is the belief that the construction of temples, tombs, circles of stones, etc. with dimensions based on the dimensions of the earth is something exceptionally powerful.

The frankmasons were city builders and the megapolysomace is the esoteric frankmason art of constructing cities, buildings or temples that had the correct space dimensions to attract the demonic spirits better and be better deposits of magical energy. It was believed that the construction of certain rooms or angles inside the chambers created entrances to other universes."[38]

2. The second idea has to do with Feng Shui. This is an Oriental practice that refers to the construction of buildings following certain alignment rules, in order to reconcile the world of the spirits with that of the human beings, to take advantage of the lines of energy and power that come from the spiritual world. It surely sounds New Age, and it is. That is precisely what I refer to. We must be aware that these occult arts are not dead but have reemerged in

these last years. In the particular case of Feng Shui you only need to consult the Internet to see the great quantity of places dedicated to this form of occultism.[39]

3. To finish, I would like to suggest that you read the material written by my friend Victor Lorenzo, an Argentinean pastor who the Lord guided in discovering how a whole city in his country was totally planned and constructed by the Masons—surely following the occult arts mentioned before.[40]

I have decided to share in detail some ideas I wrote in 1993 as a contribution for the book *Breaking Strongholds in Your City* edited by Dr. C. Peter Wagner. I consider that what was discovered then is fully valid today.

INTERACTION OF THE SPIRITUAL AND THE NATURAL

"The natural is only a reflection of the spiritual, and a connection between them always exists. We who are interested in evangelism are constantly looking for better spiritual technology."

Isaiah 45:1–3 helps us realize that God reveals new information to His people, so that we can perform better in the battle and gain the victory. We can expect that if God would go before Cyrus, "His anointed," He will likely do the same for us today. He will prepare the way for us (v. 2), give us the treasures of darkness and the hidden riches of secret places (v. 3) in order to subdue nations.

The world's population is ever increasing and we are confronted with an awesome challenge—3.6 billion people who have not yet heard the gospel! However, our God is sovereign and is revealing new and better strategies so that we may reach those billions in our generation. I am convinced that spiritual mapping is one of these revelations. It is one of the secrets of God that helps us open our spiritual "radar detectors" to show us the world situation as God sees it, *spiritually,* and not as we usually see it, *naturally.*

If I were to define spiritual mapping, I would say: It is God's revelation about the spiritual situation of the world in which we live. It is a vision that goes beyond our natural senses and, by the Holy Spirit, reveals the spiritual hosts of darkness to us.

Spiritual mapping gives us an image or spiritual photograph of the situation in the heavenly places above us. What an X ray is to a physician, spiritual mapping is to intercessors. It is a supernatural vision that shows us the enemy's lines, location, number, weapons, and above all, how the enemy can be defeated.

Spiritual mapping plays the same important role that intelligence and espionage play during war. It reveals the conditions behind enemy lines. It is a spiritual, strategic and sophisticated tool which is powerful in assisting pulling down the strongholds of the enemy.

We should also take note of another part of our supernatural vision, namely, the millions of angels whom God has sent forth to minister to those who inherit salvation (see Heb. 1:14). Angels obey His calling. They are heavenly warriors who, as a disciplined army, receive their orders from heaven itself. They come to our aid and help defeat the enemy (Dan. 10:13; Ps. 91:11; Rev. 12:7).

WHO IS THE STRONG MAN?

I had been meditating considerably over the three synoptic references to the "strong man."

1. Matthew 12:29: "Or else how can one enter a strong man's house and plunder his goods, unless he first binds the strong man? And then he will plunder his house."

2. Mark 3:27: "No one can enter a strong man's house and plunder his goods, unless he first binds the strong man, and then he will plunder his house."

3. Luke 11:21,22: "When a strong man, fully armed, guards his own palace, his goods are in peace. But when a man stronger than he comes upon him and overcomes him, he takes from him all his armor in which he trusted, and divides his spoils."

My interest was drawn to the word *man*. Why was that word used so often in the Bible? Why strong *man*? Why not strong *spirit* or strong *principality* or strong *power*? Why did it have to be specifically *man*? I began to realize that God was speaking here of the interaction between human beings and the spiritual realm.

It is natural for all armies to have their leader, a captain or general who gives orders and decides what to do. That person could be called the *strong man* of the army. We know that some people have turned out to be extraordinarily wicked servants of Satan, such as Nero or Adolf Hitler. Both of them were powerful human tools for the evil one to do what he does best—steal, kill and destroy. We could accurately call them worldwide strong men.

Hence, the devil chooses those who are willing to serve him and lifts them up as leaders on earth. It is obvious that a leader can influence many people and, therefore, can cause great destruction. These human leaders act as Satan's strong men and they represent the characteristics of the principalities they serve. I believe that such strong men on earth are assigned to principalities and powers in order to serve their purposes. These people cultivate an intimate and direct relationship with the demons through their occult activities.

We have the example of the relationship between the prince of Tyre and the king of Tyre in Ezekiel 28:2 and 12. Daniel gives us another example about the prince of Persia and the prince of Greece, who were obviously spiritual beings exerting direct relationship and influence over the empires of Persia and Greece through their emperors, their earthly rulers (see Dan. 10:20).

Isaiah 24:21 says, "So it will happen in that day, that the Lord will punish the host of heaven, on high, and the kings of the earth, on earth" (NASB). Evidently the devil rules through kings of the earth. How? Undoubtedly through the intimate relationship of his dark angels with those people who choose to give themselves to Satan.

It is known that Adolf Hitler overtly participated in this process by inviting these powers of darkness to come inside him in order to make him the strong man of his time. It is also reported today that some contemporary world leaders belong to cults of the New Age or to secret societies that seek to rule the world.

Here, I would like to warn you. We do not need to identify a human being. There are times in which God allows us to directly identify a principality or power without any person in between. I suggest you follow the guidance of the Holy Spirit and not pretend that God is following you.

The concept of the strong man is an element of great importance for spiritual warfare and thus, for spiritual mapping, that has as one of its ends to identify this strong man.

How can somebody bind him and gain victory over him if he has not been identified before? Also, the Bible adds that when the strong man is armed, his goods are in peace. This reminds me of the position and the look of the serpent in the vision I shared with you in the first chapter of this book. It was an entity that acted as if it were in charge of the situation. There was no fear in it and it was resting as if it were asleep. (Later I learned that a serpent coils over itself when it has gained the victory and is no longer afraid of any enemy attack.)

It is also necessary to remember that in some cases (see 1 Samuel 17:50–51), we need the weapons of the enemy to finish him.

PRACTICAL INSTRUCTIONS FOR SPIRITUAL MAPPING

Mature spiritual mapping requires coordinated effort aimed at taking each territory. Our purpose is to do spiritual warfare to open the door for effective evangelism and positive social change.

HOW SPIRITUAL WARFARE IS WAGED

Taking into account that I consider spiritual mapping as a technique, the best thing to do is to immediately go on describing the process we have constantly used in the past to achieve what my good friend George Otis, Jr. calls "informed intercession."[41] Just as we have been doing throughout this section, we will focus our subject from the three perspectives of spirit, soul and body.

THE PLAN

Vision:
    Evangelization of the nation or a city.

Specific objectives:

1. To do spiritual mapping that enables us to know as far as possible the enemy's plans, strategies and plots in order to go into battle with intelligence and, as a result, be victorious within a minimum of time, and with a minimum of risk and loss.

2. Using the information obtained to intervene in the spiritual warfare with the purpose of defeating the powers of the enemy in order to establish the lordship of Jesus Christ in that territory.

3. If done well, the spiritual victory will result in affecting the nation through revival, reform, and social justice, all of which are caused by the free movement of the Holy Spirit in the country.

Procedure

1. We start by praying and fasting to define the territory in which we will work. It is important that the given territory be adequate in size relative to the number of people working. We have to avoid the risk of being extremely ambitious, trying to cover too much territory. If we did there would be too many elements and variables in our equation, with the subsequent danger of wearing down and eventual confusion.

2. Once the territory is defined, the next step is recruiting personnel, brothers and sisters of good testimony, filled with the Holy Spirit, wisdom and faith (Acts 6:3). It is necessary here to warn pastors, intercession leaders, and everyone who wants to participate in this activity about the need of having a life of holiness before the Lord. Sadly,

because of ignoring this issue I have seen sorrowful situations that could have been prevented by only emphasizing the truth that spiritual warfare is not a game.

3. Once the work team is ready, we start a periodical prayer and fasting program.

4. From that moment on, we are ready to divide ourselves in three teams. This is done according to our needs and the specific gifts of each member of the group.

- The ones who constitute the spiritual factor are those who have special interest in prayer—mature intercessors who know how to hear the voice of the Holy Spirit; spiritual people who recognize the value of the supernatural and pay attention to the guidance of the Spirit, even when it comes through prophecy, dreams or visions.

- The team of the historical or cultural factor. The team is mainly comprised of the ones who have ability and inclination to research. Some find it amusing to think of them as "bookworms."

- The team relative to the physical factor. In this last team the ones who participate have natural curiosity and intuition, coupled with large amounts of energy. They will be the ones who literally cross the territory, writing up inventories, observing the neighborhoods and, many times, drawing the map of the place.

- Once the groups are integrated, the teams are not allowed to communicate with each other so there is no bias in the information. This has proven to be very useful for us, because when we receive the reports from each team the coincidences in the information each has obtained from their own perspective has the function of giving great confirmation, adding credibility and certainty to our work.

• The three working teams are assigned respectively to research historical, physical and spiritual factors of the territory.

HISTORICAL FACTORS

To do the historical research, we must ask the following questions in each city or neighborhood:

A. *The name or names*

We must make a list or inventory of the names used for our territory and then ask ourselves the following questions:

• Does the name have a meaning?

• If the etymological name has no meaning, does it have any implication at all?

• Is it a blessing or a curse?

• Is it a native, Indian or foreign name?

• Does it say anything at all about the first inhabitants of that land?

• Does it describe any characteristics of the people who live there?

• Is there any relation between the name and the attitude of its inhabitants?

- Do any of these names have a direct relation to the names of demons or the occult?

- Is the name linked to any religion, belief or local cult of the place?

B. Nature of the territory

- Does this territory have any special characteristics that distinguishes it from others?

- Is the population receptive to the truths of the gospel or, on the contrary, do they offer resistance?

- Are there many or few churches?

- Do evangelistic activities render much fruit?

- Is the socioeconomic condition of the territory uniform?

- List the most common social problems of the neighborhood, such as drug addiction, alcoholism, abandoned families, corruption of the environment, greed, unemployment, exploitation of the poor, etc.

- Is there any specific area that draws our attention? For example, could we define this territory or its inhabitants with one word? What would it be?

C. History of the territory

For this job we turn to interviews, research in the city hall, in the libraries, etc. An extremely important issue here is to know which events give a clue to the birth of this neighborhood or territory and under what circumstances this took place.

- When did it originate?

- Who was its founder (or founders)?

- What was the original purpose for its foundation?

- What can we learn from the founder? The founder's religion, beliefs, habits? Were they (or he) idol worshipers?

- Are there events that have happened frequently, such as deaths, violence, tragedies, or accidents? In some places there are places that are known for what has taken place there, for example, the "death corner".

- Is there any factor that suggests the presence of a curse or of a territorial sprit?

- Are there frightening stories? Are thcy valid? What caused them?

- How far back does the history of the Christian church go in this place?

- How did it start? Was it the fruit of a specific factor?

- The list of questions is not by any means exhaustive, but it is a beginning. We must not forget the Holy Spirit will be our main helper in this.

PHYSICAL FACTORS

The physical aspect refers to significant material objects we might find in our territory. It seems that the devil, due to his unlimited pride, frequently leaves a trail behind. So it is necessary to:

- Do an intensive study of the maps available for this region, including the oldest maps and the newest maps, which allow us to identify changes. Do the streets have a particular order? Do they suggest any kind of drawing or pattern?

- Make an inventory of monuments.

- Are there archaeological sites in our territory?

- Make an inventory of statues and study their characteristics.

- What type of institutions stand out in our territory? Power institutions, social institutions, religious institutions or others?

- How many churches do we have in the territory?

- Make an inventory of the places where God is worshiped and the places where the devil is worshiped.

- An extremely important question is: Are there "high places" in our territory?

- Are there excessive numbers of bars or witchcraft centers or abortion clinics, or pornography shops?

- A thorough study of the demographics will be of great help.

- Study the socioeconomic conditions of the neighborhood, crimes, violence, injustice, pride, blessings and curses.

- Are there occult centers in the community? Does their location have any specific distribution?

In Guatemala we have a 50-kilometer road that goes to the city of Antigua, Guatemala, and along this road we have seen all sorts of cults flourish in a straight line, including: Baha'i, Jehovah's Witnesses, Islam, New Age, witch doctors, and so on. A road like this undoubtedly constitutes an occult line of power, a corridor through which demons and the demonic powers move. These occult power lines come from contamination brought to earth by the devil through curses and invocations of territorial spirits that we are now discovering. It is helpful to locate them in order to reverse the curse and make them blessings.

SPIRITUAL FACTORS

Spiritual factors can be the most important factors of all, because they reveal the real cause behind the symptoms exposed through the historical and physical research.

Those called to work in this spiritual area are the intercessors, people who are given the gift of discernment of spirits and accurately hear from God. The group of intercessors must turn to intense prayer with the purpose of knowing the mind of Christ and receiving from God the description of the spiritual status of the enemy in the heavenly places over the defined territory.

We also have some questions the intercessors need to ask that will help guide our prayers, but they cannot be a substitute for spending quality time with God on behalf of the place for which we are praying.

- Are the heavens open in this place?

- Is it easy to pray in this place? Or is there much oppression?

- Can we discern a cover of darkness? Can we define its territorial dimension?

- Are there Specific differences in the spiritual atmosphere over the regions of our territory? In other words, are the heavenly places more open or closed over different subdivi-

sions, neighborhoods or communities ii
determine with accuracy these separatio

- Has God revealed a name to us?

- Does the information we have reveal a p
  ity we can recognize?

- Has God shown us the "strong man"?

We might become discouraged by seeing all of these questions in writing, but if we confide in the work of the Holy Spirit
and God's desire to reveal His secrets, we will feel confident. This
is not a job requiring mystical people, nor is it something weird.
All we need is a work team that feels a true burden for evangelism
in a specific territory, and the rest is the guidance of the Holy
Spirit.

When we have completed the research on all three factors,
and each group has rendered its report, we have a resulting spiritual map of the heavenly realms over our territory. Now we are
ready to do spiritual warfare. We must remember that our battle
is not against flesh and blood, but against the demonic powers
that rule over people. Also, we must remember we are called to
bless the people involved, not to curse them. Lastly, remember
that Jesus Christ has already won the battle for us!

CONCLUSION

Territoriality of spirits is a fact as far as we and our church are
concerned. We have studied the subject in the Scriptures. We have
done our homework in the field. We understand that the evil
army of hell demands worship and service from its followers and
bestows evil power in proportion to their obedience.

When a territory has been inhabited by persons who have chosen to offer their worship to demons, the land has been contaminated and those territorial spirits have obtained a right to remain there, keeping the inhabitants captive. It is then necessary to identify the enemy and to go into spiritual battle, until we obtain victory and redeem the territory. Spiritual mapping is a means to identify the enemy. It is our spiritual espionage.

Spiritual mapping is not an end in itself. It is only a technique to provide knowledge for us to carry on spiritual warfare effectively.

We have no time to lose! Now is the time for the body of Christ to rise in the power of the Holy Spirit and challenge the powers of hell, destroying all its schemes and taking back the land the Lord God has given to us as an inheritance (Genesis 48:4).

9

The Task
of the Church

*O LORD our God, other lords beside thee have had domin-
ion over us: but by thee only will we make mention of thy
name.*

ISAIAH 26:13

SPIRITUAL WARFARE
(Figure 9.1)

In the previous chapters we described our enemies and why they
have become enemies. We also have studied how to discover
them. Now it is time to talk about the subject of the task of the
Church.

Ephesians 6:18 invites us to always pray "with all prayer,"
which shows us that there are different kinds of prayer. We will
apply several of them as we engage in spiritual warfare.

Experience has made the concept I call *integral warfare* develop.
That is to say, we wage the spiritual battle simultaneously in the
three areas: spirit, soul, and body. At the end of this chapter I will
discuss in detail what I consider the key to spiritual victory in the
local church.

THE HUMAN BEING AS A WHOLE	THE WORK OF THE CHURCH SPIRITUAL WARFARE
1 THESSALONIANS 5:23 **SPIRIT**	• **WARFARE PRAYER** EPHESIANS 3:10 PSALMS 103:19–20 • **BINDING AND LOOSEING** MATTHEW 18:18 • **INTERCESSION** • **PROPHETIC INTERCESSION** • **PROPHETIC ACTS** • **SPIRITUAL MINISTRY** ISAIAH 58:6
SOUL	• **PREACHING OF THE GOSPEL** MARK 1:15 • **THE DESTRUCTION OF "STRUCTURES"** JEREMIAH 1:10 COLOSSIANS 2:20 GALATIANS 4:1–9 • **HOPE** LUKE 4:16–18
BODY	• **PROPHETIC ACTS** • **MINISTRY** ISAIAH 58:7 • **CHURCH ORGANIZATION FOR EVANGELISM** EPHESIANS 4:11–13

(In the dividing column: THE TREATMENT)

(Figure 9.1)

THE SPIRITUAL REALM

Warfare Prayer

It develops according to what is said in Ephesians 3:10, NKJV "To the intent that now the manifold wisdom of God might be made known by the church to the principalities and powers in the heavenly places." Where do we find the manifold wisdom of God? In the Word of God. The power resides in praying the Word of God over the circumstances. It is the Word of God which will exercise dominion over the enemy, and over the circumstances, causing a change, a transformation. Let's remember the biblical principle:

"While we look not at the things which are seen, but at the things which are not seen: *for the things which are seen are temporal; but the things which are not seen are eternal*" (2 Corinthians 4:18).

Those things that are not seen are the spiritual, the eternal ones. Even if they are invisible, they are more real than the ones we can see (what is seen was made out of things which do not appear). The visible, physical things are called temporal by the Word, which means "subject to change".

"*By faith we understand that the world was created by the word of God, so that what is seen was made out of things which do not appear*" (Hebrews 11:3, RSV).

When the Church engages in the task of pronouncing the manifold wisdom of God—which is the Word of God—over a city, as was done by each of the prophets including our Lord Jesus Christ (see Matthew 23:37–39 and Luke 13:34–35), the process we described in Chapter 2 under the subtitle "The Responsibility of the Church," is set forth.

This desire begins in the heart of God. Then, when man receives God's vision by the Holy Spirit, and pronounces the

Word, the angels act, and the enemy has no other alternative than to flee.

When we pray the Word of God, we are involving the angels in our battle. They "do His commandments, hearkening unto the voice of His word" (Psalms 103:20).

I find a marvelous example in David's battle against Goliath. In spite of the great physical difference between the giant and the young shepherd, Goliath did not trust what he saw but turned to spiritual weapons. The end of 1 Samuel 17:43 states, "And the Philistine cursed David by his gods." David, on his side, struck a master blow when he involved God and His angels.

"Thy servant slew both the lion and the bear: *and this uncircumcised Philistine shall be as one of them, seeing he hath defied the armies of the living God*" (1 Samuel 17:36).

"Then said David to the Philistine, Thou comest to me with a sword, and with a spear, and with a shield: but *I come to thee in the name of the LORD of hosts, the God of the armies of Israel, whom thou hast defied.* This day will the LORD deliver thee into mine hand; and I will smite thee, and take thine head from thee; and I will give the carcasses of the host of the Philistines this day unto the fowls of the air, and to the wild beasts of the earth; that all the earth may know that there is a God in Israel. And all this assembly shall know that the LORD saveth not with sword and spear: for *the battle is the Lord's, and He will give you into our hands*" (1Samuel 17:45–47).

The result confirms the value of knowing that there are two hosts over the earth: God's army on the earth and His army in the heavens (see Genesis 2:1 and Genesis 32:2).

> "*So David prevailed over the Philistine with a sling and with a stone, and smote the Philistine, and slew him; but there was no sword in the hand of David*" (1Samuel 17:50).

Many people feel the need of including speaking in tongues while doing this proclamation. I believe this is very appropriate. What is said by the apostle Paul takes place, "And in the same way the Spirit also helps our weakness; for we do not know how to pray as we should, but the Spirit Himself intercedes for us with groanings too deep for words" (Romans 8:26).

We have learned that to keep a militant attitude of prayer comes as an answer to the creativity of the leaders. It is a fact that as time passes, what had proved to be a very effective prayer strategy that once caused great interest decreases in enthusiasm. The number of people that attend the prayer services diminishes. How can we maintain enthusiasm and interest? This is a common question among pastors. Dr. David Yonggi Cho gave me the following advice: "It is necessary to constantly innovate. We must develop new and different prayer strategies every so often. For example, from the Lord's Prayer we go to the Tabernacle prayer and so on."

One of the types of prayer that has proven to be more effective for us is what we call "The Seven Hours of Power." A group of brothers and sisters come from five in the afternoon to twelve midnight (without leaving the prayer grounds) and do nothing but pray in tongues united by a particular motive. Talking, reading or doing any other activity is not allowed. In fact, we lock the doors at five o'clock sharp and they are opened again after twelve midnight. It is extraordinary what God has done through these concentrated periods of prayer. Imagine if the participating group is of one hundred persons, it means the extraordinary amount of seven hundred hours of prayer!

Binding and Loosing

This type of prayer is very popular among believers. At times it is the only one done. That is why—in certain circles—we are accused of exaggeration. I believe that it is an absolutely valid activity but surely not the only one. Of course, it has its basis in the teachings of Jesus Christ in the gospel of Matthew.

> "I will give you the keys of the kingdom of heaven; and *whatever you shall bind on earth shall be bound in heaven, and whatever you shall loose on earth shall be loosed in heaven*" (Matthew 16:19).

> "Truly I say to you, *whatever you shall bind on earth shall be bound in heaven; and whatever you loose on earth shall be loosed in heaven*" (Matthew 18:18).

Much has been said about the words binding and loosing. In my continual search for the simplest and easiest way to teach, I have not found anything better than the interpretation given to us by Kenneth S. Wuest when he tells us in his translation that binding simply means 'to prohibit' and loosing means 'to permit.'[42]

Because these are legal terms, we can freely add the term *to declare.* Then, taking into account what was just said, the verse would read like this: "whatsoever you declare prohibited on earth will be prohibited in heaven: and whatsoever you declare permitted on earth will be permitted in heaven."

This is precisely what the keys of the kingdom consist of: the ability God gave to the Church (the believers) to legally permit or prohibit an action of spiritual nature on the earth.

The principle of spiritual authority begins here. We are "ambassadors" (representatives) of Christ (2 Corinthians 5:20).

I would like to add a comment about another biblical reference to the word 'bind.' "Or else *how can one enter a strong man's house and plunder his goods, unless he first binds the strong man? And then he will plunder his house*" (Matthew 12:29, NKJV).

I previously shared briefly about the concept of the strong man. I will come back to that concept to note that the Bible speaks of the need to *bind the strong man* in order to spoil his goods. Please note that binding the strong man is not done only for the sake of binding him but for a definite purpose, plundering his goods. His territory is plundered when we bring liberty through the power of the gospel to the souls of the ones who are lost (see 2 Corinthians 4:4 and Romans 1:16).

"When a strong man, fully armed, guards his own palace, his goods are in peace. *But when a man stronger than he comes upon him and overcomes him, he takes from him all his armor in which he trusted, and divides his spoils*" (Luke 11:21, 22, NKJV). Surely you and I know whom the Word refers to when it speaks of one who is "stronger": Jesus Christ.

Let's notice that while Matthew uses the word 'bind,' Luke speaks of overcoming. It is interesting that they find these two concepts similar. I did not say they were synonyms, but similar. The situation is that when you bind the strong man you overcome him. Binding is the legal term that declares his activity as prohibited—which only confirms what Christ already did at Calvary:

"*And having spoiled principalities and powers, he made a show of them openly, triumphing over them in it*" (Colossians 2:15).

So when he is bound, he is defeated (surrendered, powerless, annulled) and we can proceed to assail him and plunder his goods.

I will tell you a story. I traveled with my wife to Buenos Aires, Argentina, to participate in a conference. The night we got there we met a friend named David Thompson. As we spoke, I asked him about Carlos Annacondia "whom I would like to greet," I said. David answered, "That will be very easy because Carlos is having a crusade near here." We went to the place, met Carlos, and had a good conversation with him. That day, God used him greatly to open my mind to the concept of the conquest. "I don't agree with having so many conferences on spiritual warfare," Carlos told me, "because they only talk and talk about binding the enemy but they don't follow through and conquer." Sensing that I was about to receive direction from the Lord, I fixed my attention on Carlos and invited him to continue his explanation. "What do you mean by conquest?" I asked. He replied, "When you bind the strong man, the next step is the conquest. When we have a crusade in a given city, a moment comes when the city has been shaken and the kingdom of the devil has been bound. That is the moment to conquer."

He was referring to evangelism, the salvation of souls, the gathering of the harvest. All these concepts are synonyms. That is what Matthew 12:29 refers to.

Let me recapitulate. We have mentioned four different concepts:

1. Discerning the identity of the strong man is done through spiritual mapping.

2. Once identified, we enter the conflict, the clash of powers, in which the enemy is bound and defeated in the name of Jesus. It is important to know that this is not a contest to see who wins. Christ already defeated the enemy and his demons, and already gave us authority over all power of the enemy (Luke 10:19).

3. Once the strong man is bound/defeated, it is necessary that we get organized in order to overcome him and divide his

spoils. We have to develop an aggressive evangelistic and discipleship mentality in order to gather and keep the harvest. And finally,

4. Do not forget to "take from him all his armor in which he trusted." Here is where we find the concepts of *hupsoma*, *logismos* and *stoicheion*, structures, ideologies, culture and others, that have to disappear when we are transformed by the renewal of our mind by the Word of God (Romans 12:2; Galatians 4:3; 4:8–9; Colossians 2:8).

Intercession

This is the labor of one who prays, calls upon the Lord, and wages the battle on his knees. It is so called because we are not praying for ourselves but for something or someone else. We could say it is an unselfish prayer. We do not pray for ourselves but instead, we are willing to be used by the Holy Spirit to pray according to His will (Romans 8:26). I especially like the statement, "Be willing for the Holy Spirit to use our prayer, our lips and all our being for His service." By definition, intercession means praying for someone or for something else. When I refer to someone else, I mean of praying for another person or persons. When I speak of something else, I refer to praying for a specific thing. For example, there are many who pray for their church or for a particular circumstance in their society, or they pray for the effects of a tragedy, such as a hurricane or an earthquake. Of course, in the end, we will be praying for people, but because of our subject, it is important to point out the difference. For example, it is very common to find believers called by God to intercede for a city or a nation. The job of the Church is to stand in the gap in favor of the earth and its inhabitants.

> *"And I searched for a man among them who should build up the wall and stand in the gap before Me for the land, that I should not destroy it; but I found no one"* (Ezekiel 22:30).

I am impressed by the fact that there are only two things that God looks for: true worshipers who worship in spirit and truth (see John 4:23), and intercessors. But what really impresses me is that He cannot find them.

> *"And He saw that there was no man, and was astonished that there was no one to intercede; then His own arm brought salvation to Him; and His righteousness upheld Him"* (Isaiah 59:16).

And, of course, we cannot forget the classic scripture of the calling and reward for the prayer on behalf of cities and nations. "[If] My people who are called by My name humble themselves and pray, and seek My face and turn from their wicked ways, then I will hear from heaven, will forgive their sin, and will heal their land. Now My eyes shall be open and My ears attentive to the prayer offered in this place. For now I have chosen and consecrated this house that My name may be there forever, and My eyes and My heart will be there perpetually" (2 Chronicles 7:14–16).

If God calls us to pray and intercede it is only because of His desire to bless and have communion with us.

"For the eyes of the Lord move to and fro throughout the earth that He may strongly support those whose heart is completely His" (2 Chronicles 16:9).

As you might remember, in Chapter 5, I showed that the natural language of the kingdom of God is intercession. You will also remember it being the task Jesus continues to do on our behalf even today (Romans 8:34).

Practical Recommendations

I would like to submit to you a number of recommendations based on my experience about this subject as Pastor of a praying church.

- On several occasions pastors have approached me and expressed the idea that for them, the intercessors have become a problem because they want to exercise too much influence upon the pastor, or because "they want to run the church." Sadly, that situation can happen, and as a matter of fact it does take place (probably too often), but I have noticed that the reason for this is the absence of the pastor during the prayer meetings. I know that some think intercession is a gift only certain people have. Let me tell you that I totally disagree with that idea. Intercession is a normal activity for believers. It is as natural as speaking or breathing. It is, I repeat, the language of the kingdom to which we belong. Some pastors do not want to get involved in this task. They delegate it to some sisters who have the gift of interceding, as if it were something too feminine for men to take upon themselves. This way of thinking is more the product of a *macho* culture, the result of the empire of the queen of heaven in some countries. We all—listen to me carefully—we all have the calling to be intercessors. If the pastor or leader wants to avoid problems with the intercession group, he will have to be an essential part of it. Only his presence will bring balance to the group.

- On the other hand, I have found that many people want to be intercessors and simply do not know how. The school of prayer is a fundamental part of any Christian church. Every pastor should dedicate a considerable amount of time teaching and practicing such a necessary ministry. Today there are many ways of learning and there is no excuse for the lack of a prayer ministry.

- I want to add that, to ensure the success of an intercessory group in the church, it is necessary for the pastor to be directly involved. Clear and open lines of communication between the leadership and the intercessors have to be in place. If they feel they are making an effort that is not appreciated, that nobody listens or pays attention to them, you are ensuring a failure. In my case, the members of our intercessory group know that I am available for them all the time. If they cannot communicate something to me during our weekly prayer meeting (as I write we are holding three meetings per week), they can call me at the office or my house at any time and tell me what they have received from the Lord.

- We have had our intercessory group even before our church started. As a matter of fact, we believe the conception of the church took place in the intercession room. We have been meeting weekly to pray and seek the Lord for many years now and are convinced that everything we have in the ministry, and many things that have taken place in our country, are a direct result of this prayer group. I cannot imagine an ecclesiastical scenario without intercession.

- I have to stress the importance of being open to the Holy Spirit and His manifestations. The more careful attention we give to the supernatural, to visions, dreams, and words of prophecy, the greater the confidence of the intercessors, which invariably results in higher dimensions each time.

As an example, I will share one of many testimonies. I was preaching in Malaysia, and from the very moment I reached that precious nation, I began to experience great spiritual oppression. As I had done many other times, I immediately called for reinforcement from our intercessory group. I called Cecilia, my wife, and sent her an SOS: "I need help. Please, call the intercessors." Cecilia—who is part of that group—transmitted my request. Immediate action was taken in the form of prayer and fasting. Approximately 24 hours later, I received a fax with the details of a vision the Lord had given one of our intercessors. God Almighty had shown her that in the nation where I presently was, there was a city called Melaka, where the Spanish conquistadors had come. They had pronounced a curse that I was to break. In the vision, the sister had seen a Spanish galleon, a hill that had a fortress in the summit, and a statue. I must confess that in that occasion I felt surprised and even a little confused. There was an element that seemed impossible to me. I was in the kingdom of Malaysia. I had never heard that Malaysia had ever been "conquered," so the Spanish galleon and the conquistadors made even less sense to me. After praying about it, I prepared for the next service where I would preach. Before leaving, I spoke with a sister. I asked her, "Have you heard the name Melaka?" "Of course," she answered. "It is a city in the south of the country." This gave me great hope, so I continued asking, "Do you know something about the conquistadors in that region?" "Of course," she repeated, "the Portuguese conquistadors." You can imagine the great excitement I felt. However, I had to stop the conversation to go to the meeting.

The service was a conference for about twelve hundred pastors. I sat down in the first row and I greeted the pastor next to me. "Excuse me," I said, "I would like to ask you something." So I mentioned Melaka. He answered, "Yes, Pastor. I am from Melaka, the city with a high hill with a fortress, and the statue of a Catholic missionary who came to preach the gospel. When he saw the hardness of the hearts of the inhabitants, he shook off the dust of his feet and cursed the region." Immediately after, he handed me documents he had prepared for me, with a detailed map of the city, the hill, and the fortress. Imagine my surprise! I preached that Saturday afternoon and three times the following Sunday. On Monday morning I was supposed to leave Malaysia and go to Singapore. Something else happened to me that day. While the plane left the airport in Kuala Lumpur, I could literally feel how the spiritual oppression started to lift. I knew that surely I could not leave that region without confronting the source of that oppression.

That same Monday night our three-day conference in Singapore began. That night I recruited people who would pray and fast and some mature intercessors to go with me the next day to Melaka. Early Tuesday morning we made our way (by car) to what ended up being a very impressive trip. When we entered Melaka, the first thing I noted was the similarity with the power centers in my own city. Even the names of the principalities (like *Santiago*) coincided. When we parked the car in a public parking lot to walk to the fortress, in front of us was a monument, a Portuguese galleon that, as you can imagine, looked a lot like the Spanish galleons. We climbed the hill and prayed as the vision had shown we should. I would like to add that I knew those actions would have supernatural effects not only for Malaysia but also for Guatemala. In the future, I will write about the great significance of that prayer. It led us to discover *Santiago*, one of the most important principalities of all those territories conquered by the Spanish Crown. As a matter of fact, we have identified it as "The

Conquistador," which went before the queen of heaven to secure its entry to new territories.

- I have seen different ways of interceding and I find a lot of them to be appropriate because they respond to the particular culture of each group or church. Nevertheless, I would like to recommend that every intercessory group have the leadership of one or more mature persons in the Lord, who has enough knowledge of the Word to be able to discern what is received. One of the weapons of the enemy consists in producing a fascination with the subject of demons and the supernatural. If you do not have that solid and mature leadership, there is a risk of falling into his schemes.

- Lastly, I want to share another recommendation that has been very beneficial to us. We have three different intercessory groups. There is a basic one that allows us to identify the areas of gifting in the ones that participate and above all, the ones interested in intercession. The second group, more specialized in a way, serves the purpose of an intensive training, and a third, more intensive group that consists of around twenty-two persons, including my wife and me. With time, we have come to develop a very close relationship with ample communication. I do not hide anything from that group. I can ask them for prayer about ministerial or personal issues with the same ease. We all share the same vision and the same desire to see our nation transformed.

Prophetic Intercession

Prophetic intercession takes place when there is a marriage between the priesthood and the prophetic. In the Bible, the priest is the figure that presents the needs or interests of the people before the Lord. The prophet, on the other hand, presents the interests of God to the people. Our Lord Jesus Christ is our model *par excellence.* In one same minister, He brings together the priest and the prophet and enunciates the principle of prophetic intercession like this, "Thy kingdom come. Thy will be done, on earth as it is in heaven" (Matthew 6:10).

Prophetic intercession is born in the heart of God because it has His will as its basis. Earlier in the book, we made reference to praying the (written) Word of God. In this case, we pray the will of God for people and/or nations. It can be praying the Scriptures or praying the words of prophecy God has spoken over a person or a nation. Many times we have experienced hearing the voice of God about a given situation, because God is interested in changing that situation and rejoices using us as His co-laborers (see 1 Corinthians 3:9 and 2 Corinthians 6:1).

Confession is a divine method for change and transformation. Remember that it is God who *"calls those things which do not exist as though they did"* (Romans 4:17, NKJV).

The difference from the intercession we normally do is that, in this one, we pray for a person. We place ourselves in the gap. Prophetic intercession however, involves another element. It is God who takes the initiative and puts the prophetic burden upon you or any of the others, to bring it into existence—to literally bring it from the spiritual to the physical realm.

THE SOUL REALM

Even if some people consider spiritual warfare as something that refers exclusively to the area of the Spirit and prayer, I believe that the mind of man is one of the most important fields where spiritual battles take place. That is why we will make emphasis on the spiritual strategy at the soul level.

The Preaching of the Gospel

Most of the activity of the Church has almost exclusively developed around this subject: the preaching of the Word. Great temples are constructed to gather people in order to preach the gospel to them. Television studios and radio stations are built for this same purpose. Why? Because the message is the vehicle through which we transmit the power of God, who saves, heals, and transforms lives (see Romans 1:16 and 1 Corinthians 1:21).

The Word of God has power (Hebrews 11:3 and 4:12) and it becomes our fundamental weapon "for pulling down strongholds, casting down arguments and every high thing that exalts itself against the knowledge of God, bringing every thought into captivity to the obedience of Christ" (2 Corinthians 10:4–5, NKJV).

The preacher has the sword of the Sprit in his hands (Ephesians 6:17), which he uses to destroy the strongholds in the minds of people. From the time I was born again, I received the teachings of a great servant of God, John Osteen. He was the one who transmitted to me the value of the Word. Under his ministry I learned to respect the Bible as the Word of the living God. I know this has been the element that has strengthened our church. Even before teaching the Bible, it is important that the pastor teach his congregation the value of the Word. When a congregation respects and values the Word, it will be willing to renounce any argument if the Bible demands it. It is the way of pulling down arguments and high things.

The preacher then has in his hands (and in his mouth and heart—Romans 10:8) the tool given by God to renew the understanding of his congregation and transform their lives. One of

God's ministers told me one time: "A preacher can mold the way a congregation thinks." How marvelous that when the Word of God is preached people are transformed into the image of Christ! (Romans 8:29).

"Therefore putting aside all filthiness and all that remains of wickedness, *in humility receive the word implanted, which is able to save your souls*" (James 1:21).

According to the gospel of Mark, in his first public appearance Jesus said, "The time is fulfilled, and the kingdom of God is at hand; *repent and believe in the gospel*" (Mark 1:15).

Repentance means to change direction, a total change of course (if I was going north, now I will go south), a change of mentality or way of thinking. Jesus Christ told them,

1. The time determined by God has come.

2. As a consequence of that, the kingdom of God has drawn near.

3. Therefore, change your mentality, change your way of thinking.

4. Instead of what you used to think and believe, now "believe the gospel."

Do not forget that the gospel is exactly opposite of the way the world thinks. While the world says, "Seeing is believing," the kingdom says, "Believe and you shall see." While the world says, "If you want to enjoy life, take everything you can," the Bible says, "For whoever wishes to save his life shall lose it, but whoever loses his life for My sake, he is the one who will save it" (Luke 9:24). That is why Jesus called us to repentance—to change our way of thinking and challenge us to believe the gospel. This is the task of the preacher, to use the sword of the spirit—the Word of God—to constantly challenge the congregation to let go of the world's way of thinking and learn not to think beyond what is written (1 Corinthians 4:6, NKJV).

When strongholds, arguments and high things are removed, the mentioned *hupsoma* and *logismos* will also be removed together with the cosmic powers that promote them.

Destruction of "the Structures"

"See, I have this day set you over the nations and over the kingdoms, to root out and to pull down, to destroy and to throw down, to build and to plant" (Jeremiah 1:10, NKJV).

In this scripture we find a strong warning for the believer. As Israel of old, we find ourselves in a hostile territory. Sadly, some act as if they did not know it.

"We know that we are of God, *and the whole world lies in the power of the evil one*" (1 John 5:19).

I am surprised at the great candidness some believers show. A group decides to plant a church and they proceed as follows: They find a place, paint it, fix it, buy musical instruments, and wait for Sunday. Then, they open the new church and wait for the people to arrive and convert. It does not even cross their minds there might be spiritual forces in the neighborhood that need to be removed.

Root Out, Pull Down, Destroy, and Throw Down

Farmers know this. Nobody would think of taking a bare plot of land and immediately plant the finest seeds there. Clearly, it would be necessary to root out the weeds and shrubs, to pull down what is of no use, destroy and throw down the debris and everything that would block the new seeds. Only after finishing the cleaning process would you proceed with the sowing without risk. That is exactly what the Word of God tells us about the spiritual realities in a territory.

The first part of the verse shows us four verbs related to destruction: root out, pull down, destroy, and throw down. After studying these words in three languages, I can assure you nothing will be left after you finish this process.

This is the plan of God regarding the mental structure we find in the world.[43] In the same manner God gave orders to the children of Israel when they entered Canaan—prohibiting them from receiving the pagan influence of the place or imitating their ways. For doing so they had previously been expelled from their land—He commands us today to root out, pull down, destroy, and discard every mental structure contrary to the Word of God.

"Do not defile yourselves by any of these things; for by all these the nations which I am casting out before you have become defiled. For the land has become defiled, therefore I have visited its punishment upon it, so the land has spewed out its inhabitants. But as for you, you are to keep My statutes and My judgments, and shall not do any of these abominations, neither the native, nor the alien who sojourns among you (for the men of the land who have been before you have done all these abominations, and the land has become defiled); so that the land may not spew you out, should you defile it, as it has spewed out the nation which has been before you" (Leviticus 18:24–28).

Many times I hear of people who are surprised because God sent Israel to war, to overcome and to eliminate the pagan nations. The exact answer lies in the scripture above. Their sin brought them to that sad consequence. Israel was only the arm that executed the judgment they had brought upon themselves.

"Elementary Principles" of the World (Stoicheion)

Once and again, the Bible speaks to us about the need we have to substitute or replace the elementary structures and the orders that are based in the world system so that we can really live the new life of freedom Christ has provided for us.

"Now I say, as long as the heir is a child, he does not differ at all from a slave although he is owner of everything, but he is under guardians and managers until the date set by the father. So also we, *while we were children, were held in bondage under the elemental things of the world. But when the fullness of the time came,* God sent forth His Son, born of a woman, born under the Law" (Galatians 4:1–4).

"However at that time, when you did not know God, you were slaves to those which by nature are no gods. *But now that you have come to know God, or rather to be known by God, how is it that you turn back again to the weak and worthless elemental things, to which you desire to be enslaved all over again?*" (Galatians 4:8–9).

"*See to it that no one takes you captive through philosophy and empty deception, according to the tradition of men, according to the elementary principles of the world, rather than according to Christ*" (Colossians 2:8).

"*If you have died with Christ to the elementary principles of the world, why, as if you were living in the world, do you submit yourself to decrees, such as, 'Do not handle, do not taste, do not touch!' (Which all refer to things destined to perish with the using)—in accordance with the commandments and teachings of men?*" (Colossians 2:20–22).

To Build and To Plant

The last two verbs in Jeremiah 1:10 are: to build and to plant. It is not only a matter of going around binding spirits or pulling down strongholds. It is about substituting the strongholds that are of God for ones that were not of God. We need to build and to plant the Word of God in the minds of people. It is not only a matter of eliminating a mental structure; it is about replacing it. Any psychiatrist or psychologist can tell us that a habit is not removed; it is substituted.

Hope

How do we build and plant? With hope. This is one of the most beautiful words that exists. Hope is the basis of Jesus Christ's ministry; consequently, of ours. When I am in the platform before the church, I feel the burden of the Lord upon my shoulders. I am there to make a difference in the lives of the people through the Word of God and the anointing of the Holy Spirit. I only feel satisfied when I know I have been able to inspire the hope of a new opportunity, a new day, a new blessing in their hearts. Remember that hope is the foundation of faith (Hebrews 11:1).

Our model, Jesus Christ, continually used the weapon of hope. He did not hesitate in announcing the work God would do through Him and the Word.

"And He came to Nazareth, where He had been brought up; and as was His custom, He entered the synagogue on the Sabbath, and stood up to read.

And the book of the prophet Isaiah was handed to Him. And He opened the book, and found the place where it was written, 'The Spirit of the Lord is upon Me, because He anointed Me to preach the gospel to the poor. He has sent Me to proclaim release to the captives, And recovery of sight to the blind, To set free those who are downtrodden, to proclaim the favorable year of the Lord.'

And He closed the book, and gave it back to the attendant,

and sat down; and the eyes of all in the synagogue were fixed upon Him" (Luke 4:16–21).

I am not at all surprised when I read the eyes of all of them were fixed upon Him. He was bringing the hope of a new day, a new future, and a new opportunity before them. I imagine someone like Bartimaeus thinking, "There is hope for the blind like me," the poor saying among themselves, "There is good news for us," the oppressed by the devil harboring the idea in their hearts of being free. This is the most marvelous message that exists. Good news means hope for the one in need.

THE PHYSICAL OR NATURAL REALM

Prophetic Acts

I found it difficult to place this subject. On one hand, these acts belong to the spiritual realm because they are prophetic. But, on the other hand, they relate to the natural realm because they are acts, actions, and activities we carry out, many times, in the physical territory.

The definition is the following: Prophetic acts are actions or activities we do in response to a prophetic word. Actually, they are prophecies that are acted out. The Bible provides us with multiple examples.

One of the most quoted cases is the prophet Elisha with the king of Israel and his battle against Hazael, king of Aram (Syria).

"And Elisha said to him, 'Take a bow and arrows.' So he took a bow and arrows. Then he said to the king of Israel, 'Hold the bow.' *And he put his hand on it, then Elisha laid his hands on the king's hands. And he said, 'Open the window toward the east,' and he opened it. Then Elisha said, 'Shoot!' And he shot. And he said, 'The Lord's arrow of victory, even the arrow of victory over Aram; for you*

shall defeat the Arameans at Aphek until you have destroyed them.'
Then he said, 'Take the arrows,' and he took them. And he said to
the king of Israel, 'Strike the ground,' and he struck it three times
and stopped. So the man of God was angry with him and said, '*You
should have struck five or six times, then you would have struck Aram
until you would have destroyed it. But now you shall strike Aram
only three times*'" (2 Kings 13:15–19).

As you see, it is not only a prophetic word but a physical act,
a prophetic action.

Another marvelous example is found in chapter 13 of the book
of Genesis. God had told Abraham, "Arise, walk about the land
through its length and breadth; for I will give it to you" (v. 17). And
we find that Abram "went on his journeys from the Negev as far as
Bethel, to the place where his tent had been at the beginning,
between Bethel and Ai" (v. 3). The Voice of the Torah[44] says: The
Talmud (holy book of the Jews containing the teachings of the
ancient teachers of the Law) deduces from this phrase that the fact
that a person can walk the length and depth of a property over
which he has certain rights constitutes an act of acquisition. Did
Abram have certain rights? Yes. God had given him a promise and
now Abram was exercising his faith through a possession, an acquisition walk.

Today we have many such strategies, like the prayer walks,
March for Jesus, the Cardinal Points Strategy, reconciliation
walks, etc.[45]

A marvelous example, and probably one of the clearest ones
regarding spiritual mapping and prophetic acts, is the instruc-
tion God gives his servant Ezekiel: "Now you son of man, get
yourself a brick, place it before you, and inscribe a city on it,
Jerusalem. Then lay siege against it, build a siege wall, raise up a
ramp, pitch camps, and place battering rams against it all

around. Then get yourself an iron plate and set it up as an iron wall between you and the city, and set your face toward it so that it is under siege, and besiege it. This is a sign to the house of Israel" (Ezekiel 4:1–3).

And if you thought that all the examples came only from the Old Testament, I invite you to read the following example: "And as we were staying there for some days, a certain prophet named Agabus came down from Judea. And coming to us, he took Paul's belt and bound his own feet and hands, and said, 'This is what the Holy Spirit says: "In this way the Jews at Jerusalem will bind the man who owns this belt and deliver him into the hands of the Gentiles""'" (Acts 21:10–11).

Jesus Himself performed a series of prophetic acts, and even some of His miracles were absolute prophetic acts, like transforming water into wine.

God has led us into doing a series of prophetic acts on behalf of our nation and even on behalf of our continent. We have seen wonders as a result of these "acted-out prophecies."

The Ministry

When God speaks of the ministry of the Church, He makes no distinction between the physical and the spiritual task. Rather, He speaks of only one ministry, that ministers to the needs of man from a complete point of view (spirit, soul, and body).

"Is this not the fast which I choose, *to loosen the bonds of wickedness, to undo the bands of the yoke, and to let the oppressed go free, and break every yoke? Is it not to divide your bread with the hungry, and bring the homeless poor into the house; when you see the naked, to cover him; and not to hide yourself from your own flesh? Then your light will break out like the dawn, and your recovery will speedily spring forth; and your righteousness will go* before you; the glory of the Lord will be your rear guard. Then you will call, and the Lord will answer; you will cry, and He will say, 'Here I am.' *If you remove the yoke from your midst, the pointing of the finger, and speaking wickedness, and if you give yourself to the hungry, and satisfy the desire of the afflicted,* then your light will rise in darkness, and your gloom will become like midday. And the Lord will continually guide you, and satisfy your desire in scorched places, and give strength to your bones; and you will be like a watered garden, and like a spring of water whose waters do not fail. And those from among you will rebuild the ancient ruins; you will raise up the age-old foundations; and you will be called the repairer of the breach, the restorer of the streets in which to dwell" (Isaiah 58:6–12).

I am persuaded the whole Church needs to have a strong deliverance ministry, an inner-healing ministry, and a ministry to care for the needy. This is the pattern I see in Christ. His ministry had three essential elements: preaching the gospel, healing the sick, and delivering the ones oppressed by the devil (casting out demons). By doing this He took care of the spiritual and emotional needs of the people without excluding their physical needs.

Organizing the Church for Evangelism

Obviously, the most important topic for the Church is evangelism. It is what our work is all about. It is also our main effort in spiritual warfare. I will address an issue that may sound simplistic to some. Nevertheless, because our motivation is the fulfillment of the Great Commission, I would like to emphasize that we need to be organized in order to be effective in evangelism and the assimilation of new believers. The Church needs to structure itself in such a way that allows it to "pick up and divide the spoils, after plundering the house of the strong man."

The Church has not acted shrewdly in this subject. Generally, churches are waiting for the people that do not know Jesus to come to church and then accept Christ spontaneously. That explains why we are not transforming nations yet. Evangelism is not spontaneous but the fruit of a well-coordinated effort in which each member of the Church is conscious of his/her role as a "fisher of men," a fellow-worker with God (Matthew 4:19, Mark 1:17; 1 Corinthians 3:9 and 2 Corinthians 6:1)

Do not forget that there is a divine order for the Church in which the saints are called to do the work of the ministry. The task of the ministers is to train, to coach, and to equip the saints so that they optimize their gifts and fulfill their divine calling.

"And He gave some as apostles, and some as prophets, and some as evangelists, and some as pastors and teachers, for the equipping of the saints for the work of service, to the building up of the body of Christ; until we all attain to the unity of the faith, and of the knowledge of the Son of God, to a mature man, to the measure of the stature which belongs to the fullness of Christ" (Ephesians 4:11–13).

I do not justify spiritual warfare at a strategic level if the target is not evangelism. Please remember that spiritual mapping is not an end in itself but only a tool to conduct efficient evangelism.

Today there is a great amount of literature available to all on cell groups and other growth groups, as well as discipleship.

CONCLUSION

The Key to Spiritual Victory in the Church

There is a strategy I consider to be the key to optimizing our resources and securing a great harvest. It is the coordinated action of the principles we have learned, applied to the local church. Firstly, we carry out our mapping investigation to define and identify the powers and structures we face. Once this is done, we prepare our strategy for church services, especially Sunday services. We share this information with the intercession groups. For example, if we are going to come against the spirit of adultery and fornication, intercessors will bind those spirits and the mental strongholds (in ideas, as well as the cosmic powers behind them) as I preach the Word perfectly synchronized with what they are praying. In this particular example, I would be preaching about marriage, family, and holiness. In this way we would be simultaneously attacking in both flanks. Lastly, the counselors are ready to receive the people when we make the altar call at the end of the service and they can minister salvation, forgiveness, deliverance, and everything else that needs to be done. Thus, we cover all three areas and defeat the enemy. There is a complete support team to work with assimilating new believers and ministering to their needs. It was very exciting to apply this strategy and watch one hundred, one hundred forty and even two hundred thirty people being added to the church each week.

Of course, you understand now that this is not a one-person job. This is exactly the reason we are a body (Ephesians 4:16).

10

The Results

Therefore, putting aside all malice and all guile and hypocrisy and envy and all slander, like newborn babes, long for the pure milk of the word, that by it you may grow in respect to salvation

(1 PETER 2:1–2).

In this chapter we will discuss the last three parts of the diagram and describe what the battle produces in the world of the spirit, soul, and body. Afterwards, we will gain wisdom and understanding from the example of Christ's ministry and that of His apostles.

THREE KINDS OF ENCOUNTERS
(Figure 10.1)

We have all rejoiced when we see a person walking down the church aisles to receive Christ. However, we are probably not conscious of all factors involved in such a decision.

As preachers, we can tell when a service is easy and smooth, or, on the contrary, we can detect resistance against the Word we preach.

Why is it that one day many come to Christ and the Word is

THE HUMAN BEING AS A WHOLE	W H A T I T P R O D U C E S	THE BATTLE	THE MINISTRY OF JESUS CHRIST
1 THESSALONIANS 5:23 **SPIRIT**		CLASH OF POWERS	**PRAYER MINISTRY** MARK 1:35 AND EVEN TODAY: ACTS 7:25
SOUL		CLASH OF TRUTHS	**MINISTRY OF PREACHING AND TEACHING** MARK 1:14–15 MARK 1:21–22 MARK 1:38 LUKE 4:16–18
BODY		CLASH OF LOYALTIES	**MINISTRY OF HEALING AND DELIVERANCE** MARK 1:23–31 MARK 1:32–34 ISAIAH 58:6–7

(Figure 10.1)

received and the next we encounter resistance? It is due to invisible spiritual dynamics that are present every time there is preaching going on or the Word is shared. The same dynamic applies whether we preach to an audience of five thousand or to a single person.

This spiritual dynamic consists of three elements I call clashes or encounters that take place at the spirit, soul, and finally, body levels.

POWER CLASHES

It is in the spiritual area that these power clashes take place. I define them as the encounter that takes place between the powers of the evil one and the power of God and His angels. It is the encounter between light and darkness and this is the outcome we can expect.

"And the light shines in the darkness, and the darkness did not comprehend it" (John 1:5).

There is little we can do in this area. However, I need to repeat that action is produced when the believer opens his mouth to express the Word of God, either when we pray, intercede, prophesy, or when we take authority over the enemy and his forces.

People have relatively little problem with this clash of powers. If I am casting out a demon, every brother will agree with me and support me in prayer. Truly, even if we refer to non-believers, the power of God is so superior to the adversary's that it presents no difficulty. Our collaboration is reduced to believing with faith in the gospel and speaking the Word of God.

The effect of prayer, intercession, and prophetic intercession provokes the clash of powers that takes place in the heavenly places.

CLASH OF TRUTHS

Some synonyms of the word *clash* are *collision, crash, impact, encounter.* The Merriam Webster Dictionary[46] defines the noun *impact* as "a forcible or enforced contact between two or more things." I find that the clash of truths can end up being more violent for us than the clash of powers, especially because of religion. The clash of truths consists of the collision that takes place between the truth of the Word of God and the truth that one believes.

As I said before, if I am casting out a demon, the entire congregation would undoubtedly support me. On the other hand, if while preaching, I speak of a controversial subject, I am confronting other people's beliefs. Even if they are believers, friends and brothers, the clash produced can be very violent and have unpleasant consequences.

An even stronger encounter is provoked when the issues being shared are of a religious nature. More than once I have perceived how strongly a person or a group can react when you present a concept that contradicts their way of interpreting God or the Scriptures. I have been dismissed from more than one Bible study or church for presenting a different vision from theirs in subjects that are common to us, like being filled with the Holy Spirit or hearing the voice of God.

Renewing our understanding through the Word of God can end up being a very difficult task. Why? Because our way of thinking, our mentality, is made up of arguments, ideas, concepts, and strongholds.

Man becomes the product or consequence of his thoughts. "For as he thinks within himself, so he is" (Proverbs 23:7).

Because of the existing need to renew our understanding, every pastor will find resistance in the minds of people, due to strongholds that have been anchored in their lives—sometimes for many years. Any pastor knows that it is easier to train children and youth in the Word of God than older people. The older a person is, the longer the time strongholds have had to take root in his/her soul. My advice for a pastor is to begin by teaching his congregation the value of the Word of God as an element of final decisions.

Matthew 24:35, Mark 13:31 and Luke 21:33 hold the same truth. God says, "Heaven and earth will pass away, but My words shall not pass away."

The preaching of the Word will generate a clash of truths. What a person thinks is confronted with what the Word of God says. Therefore, the mental structures shake, and—if we are successful— will be destroyed (2 Corinthians 10:3–5) and replaced by the Word of God—a way of thinking aligned with the Bible and the guidance of the Holy Spirit.

CLASH OF LOYALTIES

Voluntary Alignment to One of the Kingdoms

The clash of truths demands a decision. This is precisely the result of the free will God has given us. We have the capability of deciding. We can exercise our will (as I mentioned in Chapter 4), giving our loyalty to one of the kingdoms.

If I decide to change my way of thinking or living—for example, if I decide to forsake sin, I will be giving my loyalty to the kingdom of God. If, on the contrary, somebody who has known Jesus Christ decides to persist in his sinful ways, he will be exercising his will to give his loyalty to the kingdom of darkness.

Remember the concepts we shared in Chapter 4: *What a man decides and does reinforces the kingdom to which he has given his loyalty.*

But there is a need to explain that, while the preacher presents his message and then requests a decision, there are many invisible factors working simultaneously. Sometimes a person cannot get free from a habit, vice or sin. He listens to the preaching, believes the Word, but is not capable of acting upon what he believes is right. To say it in the words of the apostle Paul, *"For that which I am doing, I do not understand; for I am not practicing what I would like to do, but I am doing the very thing I hate"* (Romans 7:15).

The phrase "I do not understand" is very revealing. The person only perceives that he cannot change but does not know why. We have already learned in the last chapter that in many cases, it is not only about strongholds but also about high things (which are cosmic powers translated into ideas that try to separate man from God). Therefore, a clash of truths is not enough to produce loyalty to God and renouncement of the devil. A clash of powers is necessary. (In some cases there will even be the need of deliverance.)

That is why I emphasize the need to carry out an integral strategy. One group is dedicated to praying, interceding, and binding the powers while the preacher is dedicated to expounding the Word of God. This keeps the powers and the strongholds "in check" at the same time, and facilitates the decision of loyalty. I cannot fully explain the value of a continual intercession group during each church service.

I am personally persuaded that the church has to have a deliverance ministry available so that all the members who want it may receive it.

THE MINISTRY OF JESUS CHRIST
(Figure 10.1)

I want to show you that the Word teaches us that during His earthly ministry, Jesus dominated the enemy in the three battlefields and exercised specific activities in each of these areas.

In the Realm of the Spirit

One time I had the blessing of ministering in the city of Rosario, Argentina, and God in His mercy allowed me to participate in one of the most supernatural services I have witnessed. I saw a full demonstration of the ministry of Jesus. I was particularly tired after a week of services in Buenos Aires. As if this was not enough, we arrived in Rosario precisely when our first service started. After the service, we taped two television programs and I had about one hour to prepare for the next service. I was also a little sad because the night before our son David had been born and I had not been able to be in Guatemala accompanying Cecilia during childbirth—as I had done with our three older children. To put it mildly, it had been a difficult day but God was, once again, rich in mercy towards me.

When the service started I had a vision in which I saw the heavens open and the power of God descending over the congregation. God directed me to the first chapter of the gospel of Mark and while I preached the Word—by inspiration of the Holy Spirit—I must confess that the person receiving the most was myself. I understood the three areas of the ministry of Christ and why He was so effective. That day I saw Him saving the lost, healing the sick, delivering the oppressed, and I witnessed many miracles. I will never forget something that happened during the service. I had a word of prophecy for a woman who was bound by prostitution because of a covenant she had made with Satan. "Tomorrow," I admonished, speaking to the woman I felt was in the congregation, "look for the pastor and ask him for prayer to be free." An instant later, I had before me a young woman, who said, "I am the woman you are talking about. I cannot wait until tomorrow. I need to be free today." When she finished praying her prayer receiving Christ as her Savior, she fell under the power of the Spirit. Nobody touched her. It was the Spirit of the Lord. When she stood up, she prayed in other tongues by the Holy Spirit. It was something glorious. Her face changed, she was a new person. We had witnessed in a few minutes the clash of powers, of truths and of loyalties resulting in a glorious conversion. That is the ministry of Christ.

The Ministry of Prayer

The teaching of Christ consists of showing us that someone who desires authority and power has to have an intimate communion with God through prayer. This is called *ministering to the Lord*. It is a time in which we put our life on the altar of God. That is where we find the power to bind and overcome the forces of the enemy.

> "And in the early morning, while it was still dark, He arose and went out and departed to a lonely place, and was praying there" (Mark 1:35).

> "And when day came, He departed and went to a lonely place; and the multitudes were searching for Him, and came to Him, and tried to keep Him from going away from them. But He said to them, 'I must preach the kingdom of God to the other cities also, for I was sent for this purpose.' And He kept on preaching in the synagogues of Judea" (Luke 4:42–44).

Not only did Christ pray when He was on the earth but He continues exercising that glorious ministry even today.

"Hence, also, He is able to save forever those who draw near to God through Him, since He always lives to make intercession for them" (Hebrews 7:25).

In the Realm of the Soul

It was in the secret place, in intimate communion with God, where Jesus received instructions from God. That is where He prepared to minister to the people.

"And after John had been taken into custody, Jesus came into Galilee, preaching the gospel of God, and saying, 'The time is fulfilled, and the kingdom of God is at hand; repent and believe in the gospel'" (Mark 1:14–15).

"And they went into Capernaum; and immediately on the Sabbath He entered the synagogue and began to teach. And they were amazed at His teaching; for He was teaching them as one having authority, and not as the scribes" (Mark 1:21–22).

"And He said to them, 'Let us go somewhere else to the towns nearby, in order that I may preach there also; for that is what I came out for'" (Mark 1:38).

"And He came to Nazareth, where He had been brought up; and as was His custom, He entered the synagogue on the Sabbath, and stood up to read.

And the book of the prophet Isaiah was handed to Him. And He opened the book, and found the place where it was written, 'The Spirit of the Lord is upon Me, because He anointed Me to preach the gospel to the poor. He has sent Me to proclaim release to the captives, and recovery of sight to the blind, to set free those who are downtrodden, to proclaim the favorable year of the Lord'" (Luke 4:16–19).

In the Realm of the Body

We see the result of the ministry to God in the ministry of power towards the people. Salvation, healing, and deliverance are the characteristics of Christ's ministry.

> *"And just then there was in their synagogue a man with an unclean spirit; and he cried out, saying, 'What do we have to do with You, Jesus of Nazareth? Have You come to destroy us? I know who You are—the Holy One of God!' And Jesus rebuked him, saying,* 'Be quiet, and come out of him!' And throwing him into convulsions, the unclean spirit cried out with a loud voice, and came out of him. *And they were all amazed, so that they debated among themselves, saying, 'What is this? A new teaching with authority! He commands even the unclean spirits, and they obey Him.' And immediately the news about Him went out everywhere into all the surrounding district of Galilee. And immediately after they had come out of the synagogue, they came into the house of Simon and Andrew, with James and John.* Now Simon's mother-in-law was lying sick with a fever; and immediately they spoke to Him about her. And He came to her and raised her up, taking her by the hand, and the fever left her, and she waited on them" (Mark 1:23–31).

> *"And when evening had come, after the sun had set, they began bringing to Him all who were ill and those who were demon-possessed. And the whole city had gathered at the door. And He healed many who were ill with various diseases, and cast out many demons; and He was not permitting the demons to speak, because they knew who He was"* (Mark 1: 32–34).

> *"Is this not the fast which I choose, to loosen the bonds of wickedness, to undo the bands of the yoke, and to let the oppressed go*

free, and break every yoke? Is it not to divide your bread with the hungry, and bring the homeless poor into the house; when you see the naked, to cover him; and not to hide yourself from your own flesh?" (Isaiah 58:6–7).

THE MINISTRY OF THE APOSTLES
(Figure 10.2)

In one single scripture we can see that the apostles had understood the truths that we have spoken of and applied them in each situation they encountered.

"Now in these days when the disciples were increasing in number, the Hellenists murmured against the Hebrews because their widows were neglected in the daily distribution. And the twelve summoned the body of the disciples and said, 'It is not right that we should give up preaching the word of God to serve tables. Therefore, brethren, pick out from among you seven men of good repute, full of the Spirit and of wisdom, whom we may appoint to this duty. But we will devote ourselves to prayer and to the ministry of the word'" (Acts 6:1–4, RSV).

The language of the apostles speaks of the importance they placed on the spiritual. *"It is not right* that we should give up preaching the word of God to serve tables."

"But we will *devote* ourselves *to prayer* and to *the ministry of the word."*

And the result was quick to come, *"And the word of God increased; and the number of the disciples multiplied greatly in Jerusalem, and a great many of the priests were obedient to the faith"* (v. 7, RSV).

Many years ago, when I started my walk in the Lord, I had an experience that marked my future. We used to carry out activities like evangelistic crusades. We had a sister in the group who really did not have management skills, and was not a good organizer, but she was excellent in prayer. When she was in charge of the activity, she used to spend days in prayer and fasting, seeming to neglect everything else in the natural. However, I soon found out that when she was in charge of the activity it was much more successful than when the organizers put more interest in the natural than in the spiritual. This is a principle very easily forgotten. It is easy to become involved in our daily work. However, prayer is a luxury we simply cannot allow ourselves to neglect.

We have reached the end of our diagram and we have established the progression we find in the ministry of Christ and His apostles:

Prayer (Ministry unto the Lord).

Preaching of the gospel, the Word of God (Ministry unto the people).

The fruit is growth we can classify as supernatural.

THE HUMAN BEING AS A WHOLE	THE MINISTRY OF THE APOSTLES
1 THESSALONIANS 5:23 **SPIRIT**	**ACTS 6:4** **"But we will give ourselves continually to prayer . . . "**
SOUL	**"And to the ministry of the word."**
BODY	**ACTS 6:7** **"And the number of the disciples multiplied greatly"** **EPHESIANS 4:11–13**

(Figure 10.2)

11

The Ministry of the
Apostle Paul

*Now concerning spiritual gifts, brethren, I do not want you
to be uninformed*
(1 CORINTHIANS 12:1, RSV).

For the kingdom of God does not consist in talk but in power"
(1 CORINTHIANS 4:20, RSV).

I want to share chapter 19 of the book of Acts with you. Here we
will find the ministry of the apostle Paul. We will examine his
strategies for spiritual warfare and victory.

The chapter begins with a journey of the apostle Paul ending
with his arrival at Ephesus. *"And it came about that while Apollos
was at Corinth, Paul having passed through the upper country came
to Ephesus" (v. 1).*

1. The first principle we find is determining the key territory
   for the taking of the nation or the city. In some cases, the
   capital of the nation is the most important and influential
   place. Such is the case in many Latin American capitals like
   Mexico, Guatemala, Lima, Buenos Aires, or Montevideo. In

other cases there are cities that without being the capitals, have greater influence in the country than the capital itself. Such is the case of New York, Sao Paulo, or Sydney. In this case, a person seeking to take a nation for Jesus Christ should fix his/her eyes on the most influential city. Notice it is not necessarily the largest city, but the most influential one. Paul was traveling through Asia Minor and he chose Ephesus—the most important and influential port in the area. As a matter of fact, Ephesus was one of the three most important cities of the Roman Empire. Another fact we need to mention is that when Paul entered the city, he could not help but see its traits. From the intersections of the streets going into Ephesus he noticed the statue of Hecate, a goddess with one body and four heads, each directed to one of the streets of the intersection. Statues of Fortune were everywhere and, of course, Artemis or Diana, the Ephesian deity (definitely a territorial spirit). It was evident that the power ruling over this area had a feminine quality. We also know that in Ephesus one of the major industries was the manufacturing of idols, silver shrines of Artemis, and magic and witchcraft writings. A perfect target for Paul and spiritual warfare.

. . . "and found some disciples" (v. 1).

2. Immediately, the Word takes us to the next verb: Find. We generally see what we are looking for. This is what I find in Paul's strategy. He wanted to find a support team. Today you would call it an apostolic or ministry team.

"(. . .) and he said to them, 'Did you receive the Holy Spirit when you believed?' And they said to him, 'No, we have not even heard whether there is a Holy Spirit.' And he said, 'Into

what then were you baptized?' And they said, 'Into John's baptism.' And Paul said, 'John baptized with the baptism of repentance, telling the people to believe in Him who was coming after him, that is, in Jesus.' And when they heard this, they were baptized in the name of the Lord Jesus. And when Paul had laid his hands upon them, the Holy Spirit came on them, and they began speaking with tongues and prophesying. And there were in all about twelve men"(vv. 2–7).

3. Without preambles, Paul goes directly to the point and asks them if they have received the Holy Spirit, demonstrating his interest in the third person of the Trinity and the baptism of the Spirit. I interpret his interest as the need to level the knowledge and revelation of the disciples in order to have one vision, and to rely upon the power of the Holy Spirit. On the other hand, we find a group of twelve brothers who prove to have humble and teachable hearts. They explain their limitations to Paul and allow him to minister to them, receiving through his ministry to them the laying on of hands to the point where they themselves spoke in tongues and prophesied. This is how Paul gathered a ministerial team and proceeded immediately to minister and train them in the art of prayer. You might ask how I conclude he taught them about prayer. From Ephesians 6:18:

"And he entered the synagogue and continued speaking out boldly for three months, reasoning and persuading them about the kingdom of God" (v. 8).

4. Paul carries on his ministry exactly in the same manner Jesus had done, presenting the only message we are given to preach—the gospel of the kingdom of God, that Kingdom

that drew near to earth and was announced by Christ as the fulfillment of the time God had predetermined according to the divine will (Mark 1:12–15).

From the very beginning of His ministry, until the last forty days that Christ was on earth (after having resurrected), this was His message (Acts 1:3).

The kingdom of God manifests itself on the earth in power. The kingdom of God exercises pressure over the kingdom of darkness. During the Old Testament days, little was known about demons and we do not have evidence of somebody taking authority and casting them out. But, when the kingdom of heaven draws near to earth, Jesus started demonstrating that the kingdom of God prevails over darkness, and a manifestation of that victory is the defeat and casting out of demons by the finger of God (Luke 11:20).

We cannot think we will enter into a territory that has belonged to the devil with our own strength or our message. The weapons that are not of the flesh, but divinely powerful in God to cast out the devil from a territory, are needed.

> *"But when some were becoming hardened and disobedient, speaking evil of the Way before the multitude, he withdrew from them and took away the disciples, reasoning daily in the school of Tyrannus" (v. 9).*

In this passage we find the first manifestation of the opposition of the enemy. (The message of the kingdom will always produce a reaction.) We have to notice the wisdom of the apostle that when he sees there is such a strong resistance and some even curse Christ (the Way), he chooses to separate his disciples, protecting them and moving to another place where he can continue his work of proclaiming his message.

It is not strange that the enemy offers resistance. We can always be assured that when the enemy raises against us as a river, the Lord will rise a banner against him (Isaiah 59:19).

5. God's reaction in favor of Paul did not tarry.

> "And God was performing extraordinary miracles by the hands of Paul, so that handkerchiefs or aprons were even carried from his body to the sick, and the diseases left them and the evil spirits went out" (vv. 11–12).

6. The second attack of the devil, more malignant than the first, did not delay either.

> "But also some of the Jewish exorcists, who went from place to place, attempted to name over those who had the evil spirits the name of the Lord Jesus, saying, 'I adjure you by Jesus whom Paul preaches.' And seven sons of one Sceva, a Jewish chief priest, were doing this. And the evil spirit answered and said to them, 'I recognize Jesus, and I know about Paul, but who are you?' And the man, in whom was the evil spirit, leaped on them and subdued all of them and overpowered them, so that they fled out of that house naked and wounded" (vv. 13–16).

7. Due to the defeat the devil suffered in his first attempt, he now turns to confusion, a more subtle way of trying to invalidate the message Paul is preaching. Alas! Let's not forget that Paul has what today we call a group of intercessors. It comes as no surprise that God transformed the

attack of the enemy into a major opportunity for blessing.
On the other hand, it will do us good to consider that the
name of Jesus has power as a result of a relationship. It is
not something automatic or magical to those who do not
know Him.

*"And this became known to all, both Jews and Greeks, who
lived in Ephesus; and fear fell upon them all and the name of
the Lord Jesus was being magnified" (v. 17).*

8. When the Apostle Paul saw God's action and noticed that
   fear had come upon the entire city, he performed what I
   call his master strike. Be it by direct guidance of the Holy
   Spirit or by Paul's invitation, confession of sins took
   place—a powerful deed if you take into account that it was
   done publicly.

*"Many also of those who had believed kept coming, confessing,
and disclosing their practices" (v. 18).*

9. Then, there was a renouncing of their former way of living
   and a decisive action of change. They brought their books
   of magic that contained spells, enchantments and recipes
   of different potions with which they practiced occultism
   "and began burning them in the sight of all," again, publicly.
   At this point I want to introduce a definition that I will
   only mention due to the fact that the same has led me to
   write a second book to expand on the two concepts that
   conform it: *'The objective of spiritual warfare is the permanent displacement of the principalities and the total elimina-
   tion of their survival systems.'*

"And many of those who practiced magic brought their books together and began burning them in the sight of all; and they counted up the price of them and found it fifty thousand pieces of silver" (v. 19).

10. Paul gave himself to the task of eliminating magic (occultism) that undoubtedly fed the principalities by granting them authority over the territory due to the flagrant violation of the Word of God. By burning the books, the enchantments, incantations, and formulas were destroyed, making it impossible to fall back into them. It was really a master blow because people were obtaining forgiveness from God while, at the same time, the principalities were suffering a great defeat, losing their source of power. We can also think that many demons (remember here the word *hupsoma*) that usually inhabit these types of books and objects were expelled. And as if that was not enough, the price of what was burned was fifty thousand pieces of silver. Remember that thirty pieces of silver, which constituted the payment Judas received for committing treason against Christ, was enough to buy a field large enough to be a burial place for strangers (Matthew 27:3–9 and Acts 1:18). What I mean is that what they burnt that day was a real fortune with which they could have bought one thousand six hundred and six of those fields! So, it was even a great financial sacrifice unto God, with an enormous cost to the devil.

"So the word of the Lord was growing mightily and prevailing" (v. 20).

11. The result was glorious. Paul won the victory and picked up the spoils. It doesn't surprise us that the principalities of higher hierarchy entered the battle.

> "And about that time there arose no small disturbance concerning the Way. For a certain man named Demetrius, a silversmith, who made silver shrines of Artemis, was bringing no little business to the craftsmen; these he gathered together with the workmen of similar trades, and said, 'Men, you know that our prosperity depends upon this business. And you see and hear that not only in Ephesus, but in almost all of Asia, this Paul has persuaded and turned away a considerable number of people, saying that gods made with hands are no gods at all'" (vv. 23–26).

12. The enemy attack is plotted through greed, something found so frequently in the devil's plans. It is not in vain that the Word of God says in 1 Timothy 6:10, *"For the love of money is a root of all sorts of evil, and some by longing for it have wandered away from the faith, and pierced themselves with many a pang."* But greed would seem to be a fairly common force if it did not come coupled with additional elements: idolatry, and the object of that idolatry, Diana of the Ephesians. Now we can understand that Paul had to fight the battle on the three levels Dr. C. Peter Wagner talks about. The first level consists of the deliverance ministry; the second deals with occultism, and the third, called the strategic level, defies the cosmic powers.

Notice that Paul also fought in the three battlefields. He destroyed the books that constituted the physical contact point with the structures and the principalities (v. 19). He confronted the structures in the minds of the people (v. 26) about idolatry, and then, challenges the principalities.

> "And not only is there danger that this trade of ours fall into disrepute, but also that the temple of the great goddess Artemis be regarded as worthless and that she whom all of Asia and the world worship should even be dethroned from her magnificence" (v. 27).

13. I find it very revealing that Demetrius fears the "magnificence," the authority of Diana might be destroyed. Which means that this principality descends from its (high) authority place. In our modern language we would say that Diana is losing strength and is about to be overthrown, because the principalities and structures that were sustaining her had suffered Paul's demolishing attack.

> "And when they heard this and were filled with rage, they began crying out, saying, 'Great is Artemis of the Ephesians!'" (v. 28).

14. It is a proven fact that idolatry produces confusion, thus using the people who, as is shown to us in the following verse, many times do not even know why they are doing what they are doing.

> "So then, some were shouting one thing and some another, for the assembly was in confusion, and the majority did not know for what cause they had come together" (v. 32).

15. In closing, we can see that Diana staggers and needs the power of praise so—knowingly or not—the confused multitude provides that principality with the source of power it desperately needs.

"But when they recognized that he was a Jew, a single outcry arose from them all as they shouted for about two hours, 'Great is Artemis of the Ephesians!'" (v. 34).

16. Now we have finished the picture. Paul has overthrown the strongholds and high things and has destroyed the points of physical contact. As a consequence, the ruling principality, Diana (of which the theologian Clinton Arnold explains that it could well have been the ruling principality over all the Roman Empire), has lost its power.

The result is absolutely supernatural:

"And this took place for two years, so that all who lived in Asia heard the word of the Lord, both Jews and Greeks" (v. 10).

We know through history that it was the apostle John who pastored the church in this city, which ended up having twenty thousand people. We also know it was the apostle John who directly defied goddess Diana and overcame her, to the point that her altar broke down in pieces and half of the temple came down to earth.[47]

Conclusion

"Now may the God of peace Himself sanctify you entirely; and may your spirit and soul and body be preserved complete, without blame at the coming of our Lord Jesus Christ."

(1 THESSALONIANS 5:23)

We have come to the end of our journey, which took us through certain truths concerning the subject of spiritual warfare. Now I want to share with you a conclusion that might become an invitation to practice these precious principles and set us in the path for the next book I am preparing.

PROPHETIC PATHWAYS

Again, I will make use of material I used for the book *The Transforming Power of Revival,* which we edited for the World Congress on intercession, spiritual warfare and evangelism held in Guatemala City, on October 1998.[48]

The 90's have been identified as the decade of prayer and spiritual warfare. Undoubtedly, God has emphasized these topics in His Church. Many of us have been privileged to participate in the worldwide movement of prayer that the Holy Spirit initiated in every continent of the world. During the last years we have learned a great deal, and I personally feel this movement has reached its maturity. I feel the moment has come to unify criteria and draw conclusions. The time has come to define strategies based on what we have learned and to let the Holy Spirit take us by the hand and launch us into the future. The church I lead and I have walked through a series of circumstances that have shaped our way of thinking in relation to intercession, spiritual warfare, and evangelism. I have traveled a path in which the Holy Spirit has challenged me once and again. It has been a continuous process of challenge, teaching, and practice, time and time again. These challenges and the fruits of constantly seeking His face have been engraved in the history of our ministry and have become teachings that the Lord has allowed me to share throughout the world.

The chronological process we have experienced shapes the order of the topics which constitute the conclusions I have come to in these years. I would like to remind you that the perspective I offer is my point of view as a local pastor. Let me lead you along the path that took us a decade.

Spiritual Mapping

Just as I told you in Chapter 1, our first exposure to the subject of spiritual warfare was due to a fortuitous finding of a pre-Columbian monument in the property of our church: the Great Snake Mound of the Valley of Guatemala. The monument was a reflection of a principality to which the first inhabitants of the land had offered their loyalty in what now constitutes the valley of Guatemala; its name was Quetzalcoatl, the flying serpent or feathered serpent.

Our country had been offered—dedicated—to this principality. What we discovered after this was even more revealing. The characteristics of this god were reflected in all of our society. This is how we discovered the principle stated by the Apostle Paul in chapter one of the book of Romans: we can perceive the invisible through the visible things.

We began to see that the physical—natural—realm is a reflection of the invisible spiritual powers that had originated in what is seen. Little by little, we became aware that the root of all the problems that plague our country coincided exactly with the "pacts or covenants" made between the early inhabitants (the stewards) of this land and the principalities they worshiped.

Immediately, we began a prayer thrust called "Jesus is Lord of Guatemala." Our mission: to enlist an army of intercessors that would pray an hour a day for Guatemala. Our goal: to redeem our nation in order to give it to Jesus Christ.

The most important conclusion we arrived at was understanding that the principalities, which by definition are disembodied spirits, cannot subdue men to slavery themselves. They must use the power that comes from the soul.

We also learned that a principality or power (Ephesians 6:12) that has certain features works by generating strongholds, arguments or arrogance (high things). In other words, it exercises its power through concepts, ideas or ideologies (2 Corinthians 10:4–5) that constitute the mentality or prevalent way of thinking in a community. I like to call this the *culture of the social conglomerate.* It is precisely this way of thinking that drags people into slavery.

Someone asked me, "What is the use of spiritual mapping?" I answered, "To know the reality we face."

Jeremiah 1:10 commands us to pluck up and to break down, to destroy and to overthrow, to build and to plant. How are we going to accomplish this if we do not know what we are dealing with?

A vital teaching was: *Spiritual mapping is not an end in itself. It is only a tool for spiritual warfare.*

Spiritual mapping is for the intercessor what an X-ray is for a doctor. It is a means to diagnose the spiritual reality that affects our communities.

Spiritual Warfare

What we learned through spiritual mapping gave us the necessary elements to pray effectively for our nation. We understood what the real needs were, what were the origins of the different problems, and above all, the elements of darkness that were keeping people in the slavery of unbelief (2 Corinthians 4:4) and which caused them to resist the gospel of Christ.

The intercession effort called "Jesus is Lord of Guatemala" experienced great blessing. The whole nation was shaken by God's answers to the prayers of the saints. We experienced huge changes in different areas of the society. We had great blessings politically, socially, and even economically in the country. God's mercy allowed us to enter the area of prophetic intercession—the marriage of the priesthood and the prophetic. We became deeply involved in prayer, fasting, and intercession for the nation.

Everything seemed to be alright until I had a conversation with a church member whom I appreciate very much. He asked me, "Have you seen that the church of such-and-such pastor is growing?" I said, "Yes, I've heard it is growing." He asked again, "Have you heard that the church of brother so-and-so is also growing?" I nodded again, but I probably was not prepared for the next question. "And why is it that we pray and pray and yet we do not grow?" I have to tell you that the question really hit the spot. This is what I call Holy Spirit "attention calls" or challenges.

I was immediately on a quest for an answer. We were certainly praying, and every battle seemed crowned with victory, but the local church itself was not growing the way any pastor would want. What was going on?

The answer was not delayed: *Spiritual warfare is not an end in itself; it is just a tool for effective evangelism.*

I have come to understand that spiritual warfare is fought on three battlegrounds:

1. *War in the air.* The battle that takes place during prayer is against principalities. This can include prayer, fasting, and intercession. But it can certainly include carrying out prophetic acts, identificational repentance, etc.

2. *War in the soul or mind of man.* This is specifically the destruction of strongholds. Here, the arguments, concepts, and high things that have risen up against the knowledge of God are disarmed.

3. *War in men's hearts.* Here it is necessary to emphasize concepts that are vital for Christ's body, such as personal holiness and the unity of the Body.

We have designed a very efficient system of fighting the battle simultaneously on these three fronts. In every service held in the church, we assign a different group for each battlefront. The intercessors and I agree in prayer before the service and they are in charge of binding Satan's powers and loosening God's anointing over the congregation that listens in the sanctuary and by radio. While they keep these spirits tied in the heavenlies, I am in charge of preaching, bringing down the strongholds in people's minds, using the sword of the Spirit—the Word of God—as a weapon. A third team made up of ministers gets ready to gather the harvest, minister salvation, deliverance, and prayer for any other need in those who respond to God's Word. I have personally noticed the great support in having the intercessors pray while I preach.

Evangelism

Any believer understands that the reason we are still "in the world" is to evangelize those who do not yet know Christ. We are not here to reach a greater level of salvation or sanctification because the salvation that the blood of Jesus Christ attained for us cannot be improved upon. What, then, is the purpose of our existence on this earth? As I said, it is what we commonly call the Great Commission (Matthew 28:19).

I understood there is a great need of joining the concepts of spiritual warfare and evangelism within the context of the local church in a practical way.

Soon—very soon—after we learned this truth we began to have a considerable number of conversions. The prayer marches, fasting periods, and intercession subjugated the powers of darkness. The strong man was bound and defeated, and we started to reap the reward. Many people found Christ in every meeting. Apparently we had found the solution. Yet, something was still missing. Many of these new believers did not return to church after their conversion. We were trying different methods, but it seemed something was still lacking.

Discipleship—Assimilation of New Believers

We sought the guidance of the Holy Spirit to organize the local church in order to grow. The plan was to integrate the concepts we had recently learned in spiritual warfare, prayer and intercession together with evangelism through the existing structure of family (cell) groups in the church. What I was discovering was nothing but the same principles that made Yoido Full Gospel Church in Seoul, Korea, become the largest church in the world under the leadership of Dr. David Yonggi Cho.

The results of combining these concepts were amazing. Soon our family groups became evangelistic groups that applied the principles of spiritual warfare in order to become effective soul winners. Now we were applying the principles of assimilating new believers. The family groups became the ideal method for us to accomplish the Great Commission locally. God did not call us to make believers; He called us to make disciples. Having a great number of conversions is not enough. It is necessary for new Christians to learn to walk the path of discipleship.

We now had the vehicle to evangelize people, and those who had received Christ proceeded to a discipleship plan and service to God, which made them evangelists. Fantastic!

We had a celebration to commemorate the achievements of the year that had just ended. When we saw the graphs projected on the screen, I could hardly contain my emotions. The growth graph clearly showed an increase in new converts every time spiritual warfare activities took place. On one occasion, in just one Saturday, when cell groups were held, more than 800 people were saved and most of them became church members. Our concepts evolved to the point where we no longer talked of people saved, but we referred to the people that had been saved and added to the church. Soon they were one hundred a week, then 120, 140, even 230 a week! It seemed like now we finally had all the elements together. But the Holy Spirit brought another challenge.

Discipleship through Christian Education

Few things impress us as much as the sovereign acts of God. Apparently, He takes advantage of every circumstance in our life to bring breakthrough, growth, and expansion to our minds.

I had a very serious problem due to the construction of our temple. Once again the conflict originated in connection to "The Great Snake Mound of the Valley of Guatemala." However, this time it was a serious legal problem that almost put me in jail. While waiting for a legal audience with the judge in charge of the case, I stayed secluded in my house for four days. It was a time of great stress, but probably one of the greater opportunities for blessing in my life.

The Lord surprised me once again. "So you want to win this nation for the gospel?" He asked me. After making sure this was the vision for my life, He added, "I will reveal to you the most powerful weapon for the taking of a nation—Christian education."

We had had a Christian school in the church for ten years. However, I must admit the vision was never in me. My wife and sister-in-law carried the vision throughout these years, but I had not received the revelation personally.

God's next two arguments were impressive. The first was making clear to me that the mistake of the Christian Church consists of "going for yesterday's generation and not for the future one." We invest in all kinds of plans for adults, yet we pay very little attention to children. The second consisted of reminding me of an experience I had long ago when I traveled to the United Kingdom.

After preaching in Nottingham, I was able to visit Wales. I had a strong desire to visit the Biblical Institute of Wales. I was motivated by two very important reasons. The first was the great impact the book *Rees Howells, Intercessor* had upon me. The second was an interest in visiting the city where the Welsh revival started at the beginning of this century.

Once again, I found myself poorly prepared for the revelation the Lord wanted to give me. Rev. Samuel Howells' assistant met me at the train station, and while he was driving me to the Institute I could see the beautiful Welsh churches. I greatly enjoy the architecture of those buildings. However, I was extremely saddened to see that some of them had been turned into restaurants, others were for sale, and some had even become Muslim mosques. To my surprise, I was informed that only one percent of the inhabitants of Wales is Christian. What a tragedy for a place that witnessed God's power in such a way that, in just six months, half a million people were converted. My conclusion was the phrase you have all heard, "God does not have grandchildren."

If we do not invest in affecting the next generation, if we do not educate children in God's Word, then every time a generational cycle starts we will again have to evangelize the children of those who were believers. This makes it very difficult to "make disciples in every nation."

I would like to ask you a very simple question. Which is easier: to pluck up and to break down, to destroy and to overthrow strongholds and arguments in people's minds or to have the mind of an infant that has not been contaminated and is ready to receive the planting of the Word of God? The answer is obvious. *Without Christian education, every revival is condemned to live for only one generation.*

Community Transformation

I was invited by brother George Otis, Jr. to preach in a congress he organized in Seattle, Washington, in November, 1997. There was great pressure on me the day I arrived. I have a strong ability to communicate whatever I believe in. But if I, myself, am not persuaded, I find it impossible to proclaim something as if it were the truth. I owe it to my natural father, who sowed a series of principles in me that I am not capable of betraying.

Precisely because of those principles, I approached George immediately and told him, "I need to talk to you before the Congress starts. I am having enormous difficulty with many things being called spiritual warfare today. When the Bible speaks of spiritual victories, the results are evident and measurable. I am concerned about spiritual warfare testimonies that lack a genuine application. The entire movement is in danger if we do not find a way to link what we do to clear, concrete and provable results."

George understood my restlessness. I think he appreciated my sincerity and, with his characteristic kindness, took a paper out of his briefcase and told me, "You are the first one I will show this document to. I am working on a concept that is born out of the same concern you have just expressed to me. I have called it 'community transformation,' and it is a way to measure the impact our prayers have in our community."

I felt a tremendous relief. It was the answer to my restlessness. We would now have a way of giving prophetic guidance to those interested in praying, interceding for and taking their cities for Christ. We now had a scale to measure the results. You will find a detailed exposition of this subject in *Spiritual Mapping Research Questions,* by George Otis, Jr.[49]

Spiritual warfare is only one aspect, a part of the gears in God's machinery to bless the earth and its inhabitants. The revival, a result of the saints' pleas, is another part of this machinery. Christian education is a way of assuring that the revival will affect future generations. The reformation and restoration of a community are ways of measuring the impact of revival.

Spiritual awakenings in the past, such as the Reformation in the 16th century and great revivals such as the one in Wales, confirm our belief that transformation is a possible, real, and tangible result of God's move. Judging by our society's condition, it is desperately necessary.

Revival and Social Impact

If we are talking about a continuous process, we would have to say that our prayers, if guided by the Holy Spirit, will be answered by God. As in Daniel's case in Daniel chapters 9 and 10, the answer will bring a move of the Holy Spirit. This is what we call a revival or awakening. If this revival we deeply desire is produced, we would have the right to hope for a lasting impact and to effect a permanent transformation.

History shows us that revivals have produced great change in every level of society. Every time that God has moved, the revival has resulted in reformation, and this reformation has brought restoration.

Revivals have brought a new awakening that, in many instances, have produced true revolutions in the areas of evangelism, Christian education and social ministry. Great universities, hospitals, and church buildings are today's witnesses of the Holy Spirit's movement in previous times.

The most important factor that stands out, however, is to verify that during a revival the gospel permeates society and its way of thinking. In other words, the enemy's strongholds, and the powers in the air that produced them, are both brought down by the power of God. While the heavens are open, the way of thinking changes, aligning itself with the Word of God. The words of Thomas Jefferson, writer of the United States Declaration of Independence, greatly impress me. He recognized that his way of thinking was a product of the society of that time, in other words, Christianity and a biblical mindset.

I am absolutely persuaded that real revival is one that produces a social effect, a transformation. In the miracle city of Almolonga, the process began (just as in Acts 19) because of discipleship and prayer. Then it was followed by a consistent practice of the deliverance ministry, thus affecting the powers of Maximon, the territorial spirit whose empire was removed (spiritual warfare), which opened the heavens, bringing a great revival (evangelism). The resulting revival transformed the life (producing eternal life) and culture (the way of thinking) of the people, changing their habits and customs. It even went so far as to affect the natural elements, making Almolonga the most fertile land in the whole country. Certainly, this is a marvelous example from God, a living proof that allows us to testify that "There is nothing impossible for God."

God's great challenge is before us. Do you want a holy transformation for your nation? I pray to God that the concepts we have shared in this book may make a difference in your life and nation.

TO CONTACT THE AUTHOR:

Pastor Harold Caballeros
El Shaddai Church
4 Calle 23-03, Zone 14
Guatemala City 01014, Guatemala
(502) 3374777
www.elshaddai.net
elshaddai@guate.net

Notes

1. Carlos Navarrete y Luis Luján Muñoz, *El Gran Montículo de la Culebra en el Valle de Guatemala* [*The Great Mound of the Snake in the Valley of Guatemala*], Universidad Nacional Autónoma de México, Academia de Geografía e Historia de Guatemala, 1986.

2. Op. Cit.

3. *La Serpiente Emplumada, Eje de Culturas* [*The Feathered Serpent, Axis of Cultures*], José Díaz Bolio, 3ª. Edición, 1964. Registro de Cultura Yucateca, Mérida, Yucatán.

4. "Judge de Pellet, Ritual Astronómico" ["Ball Game, Astronomic Ritual"], in the quoted Díaz Bolio book.

5. We give thanks to God that in Central America, the war is over, a fact we interpret as a direct answer to the intercession of the Church, and also supposes the destruction of the ties that principality had over our territory.

6. I urge you to feel free to make good use of any of the charts here to benefit other people.

7. In Romans 7:9–11, the Apostle Paul clearly states that, in the strictest sense, man begins his walk in the kingdom of light, by being created in the image of God. However, when sin makes its entrance, a moment some call the *age of conscience,* we pass to the kingdom of darkness from which we need to be redeemed.

8. Colossians 1:16 (NKJV) explains to us that in Christ "all things were created that are in heaven and that are on earth, visible and invisible, whether thrones or dominions or principalities or powers. All things were created through Him and for Him." This is to say, then, that there were principalities that became corrupt and allied with the devil, but there were others that remained faithful to God. (See Revelation 12:4, 7 and Hebrews 2:14.)

9. The book of Daniel lets us see that even if there are princes that serve the evil one—as the prince of Persia, or the prince of Greece—God also has princes that serve His children—as Michael, who has the honor of being prince over the children of Israel. (Daniel 10:20–21)

10. During the period of research, I studied Donald Grey Barnhouse's book called *The Invisible War,* which greatly blessed me in this sense, because it was the first time I saw my idea of a great parenthesis—I called it "The times of the Bible"—being confirmed.

> *The Invisible War,* The Panorama of the Continuing Conflict between Good and Evil. Donald Grey Barnhouse. Ministry Resources Library. Zondervan Publishing House. Grand Rapids, Michigan, USA.

11. One of the most important sources of information is the book *God's Plan for Man,* written by Rev. Finis Jennings Dake, Published by Dake Bible Sales, Inc., Lawrenceville, Georgia, USA.

12. *The Invisible War,* p. 26.

13. *The Invisible War,* p. 27.

14. God's relationship to man has always been a relationship of giving and receiving—an exchange. God has given us creation, natural life, Christ, eternal life, etc. And man receives what God gives him. So says the Scripture, "A man can receive only what is given him from heaven" (John 3:27). I believe this concept is especially striking, given that even at the moment of Christ's sacrifice at the cross, what took place was an exchange.

> He took our sins and our rebellions; He bore our pains, our diseases and rejection, and gave us His justice, salvation, healing, and acceptance in the Beloved.

> The doctrine called *imputation doctrine* (what was ours was upon Him and what was His came to be ours), becomes "The Divine Exchange." I heard this term for the first time on the lips of the well-known author Derek Prince, when we spoke about exchange or transaction of merchandise.

15. Even in this dispensation, God continues seeking that worship (see John 4:23).

16. *"I will make myself like the Most High"* is the climax of his ambition (Isaiah 14:14).

17. Being able to undertake a study of each of these Hebrew words, I have tried to avoid this endeavor for the reader, for the sake of making the text of our study more fluid.

18. Paul E. Billheimer, *Destined to Overcome, The Technique of Spiritual Warfare,* Kingsway.

19. Because of this, now curse, death, darkness, etc. exist. If you observe carefully, Zechariah 14:11 and Revelations 22:3–5 state clearly that there will no longer be death or curse. Neither will there be need of light of the sun because there will be no night. That is, this duality is confined to the present time, but when we again enter eternity, all these calamities, fruit of rebellion, will cease to exist. We will again have the exclusive kingdom of the "will of God."

20. Orders and structures are two words we will come back to again and again. For the time being, we will mention the word rudiments or *stoicheia.*

21. Sentence executed according to Revelations 20:10.

22. When Adam chose the other will.

23. I think it would be of great worth to the reader to read Watchman Nee's book called *Spiritual Authority*.

24. I am persuaded that the responsibility of the believers is even larger because we know the Word and know the result that our actions can provoke. This means that, for us, not only the risk itself of the "commission" exists but also the "omission" one. "Therefore, to one who knows the right thing to do, and does not do it, to him it is sin" (James 4:17).

25. On the other hand, in this part of the parenthesis in which we live, how could man decide between good and evil if there was no option of evil?

26. Watchman Nee, *The Latent Power of the Soul,* Christian Fellowship Publishers, Inc., New York, 1972, p. 29.

27. About the subject of blessings and curses, I would like to recommend the book by Derek Prince, *Blessing or Curse. You Can Choose! Freedom From Pressures You Thought You Had To Live With,* published by Chosen Books, Fleming H. Revell Company, Tarrytown, New York, USA. This book is also available in Spanish. I believe it is one of the best books on the subject.

28. Man consists of three parts: Spirit, soul and body. Each of them is subdivided in three parts, which provide feedback among each other. For example, the blood is produced in the bones. The blood is the life of the flesh (muscles), and those muscles sustain the skeleton (the bones.) Spirit: Intuition, communion and conscience.

Soul: Mind or intellect, feelings or emotions and volitional capability or will.

Body: Blood, flesh and bones.

In the same way, the ones involved in spiritual warfare interact with each other. The powers express themselves through strongholds that manifest themselves as a covering of darkness and a veil of blindness.

29. *Warfare Prayer*, C. Peter Wagner, Regal Books, (pp. 89–103; in Spanish *Oración de guerra*, Editorial Betania).

30. "Fuera de aquella región" Reina Valera, 1960.

31. See the chapter by Harold Caballeros, "Defeating the Enemy with the Help of Spiritual Mapping," in the book edited by C. Peter Wagner, Regal Books, *Breaking Strongholds in Your City.*

32. *Informed Intercession*, by George Otis, Jr., Renew, a division of Gospel Light, pp. 18–23. *The Twilight Labyrinth*, by George Otis, Jr., Chosen Books, pp. 308–311. *Confronting the Powers*, Peter Wagner, Regal Books, pp. 217–220.

33. "For as he thinks in his heart, so is he." Proverbs 23:7, NKJV.

34. *Confronting the Powers*, by C. Peter Wagner, Regal Books, (pp. 238–240. In Spanish, *Confrontemos las fortalezas*, Editorial Betania). Dr. Wagner quotes J. Blunck in *"The New International Dictionary of New Testament Theology,"* edited by Colin Brown, Zondervan Publishing House, ISBN 0-310-33238-9, 2nd Volume, (pp. 198 to 205).

35. For those interested in the subject of "Lines of Iniquity," the author has an in-depth study of the subject on a tape that can be obtained though El Shaddai Ministries, Guatemala (www.elshaddai.net).

* "Muéstranos qué hemos de decir; porque nosotros no podemos ordenar las ideas a causa de las tinieblas." Job 37:19, Reina Valera

36. When we refer to the Greek mentality, we refer to the action of the spirit called spirit of Greece, which has its cultural manifestation

through the western view of the world. Again, if the reader wishes to obtain more information about this study material, contact El Shaddai Ministries, Guatemala (www.elshaddai.net).

37. The author is completing a second book called *Kings and Priests*, where this subject is covered in detail.

38. *Lucifer Dethroned*, A True Story, by William and Sharon Schonebelen, pp. 202–203, Chick Publications. ISBN: O937958417.

39. If the reader wishes to find information about Feng Shui, an alternative would be to look for material about geomancy.

40. Víctor Lorenzo, "Evangelizing a City Dedicated to Darkness," Chapter 7 of *Breaking Strongholds in Your City* edited by C. Peter Wagner (in Spanish, "Cómo evangelizar una ciudad dedicada a las tinieblas" from the book *La destrucción de fortalezas*, Editorial Betania). Víctor Lorenzo can be reached in Osvaldo Cruz 2939 (1293), Capital Federal, Buenos Aires, Argentina. Telephone 54-11-4303-1268 or Fax: 54-11-4303-4068.

41. I recommend you read the book by George Otis Jr., *Informed Intercession. Transforming your Community through Spiritual Mapping and Strategic Prayer*. Renew/Gospel Light Books, 1999.

42. *Wuest's Word Studies* by Kenneth S. Wuest, Wm. B. Eerdmans Publishing Company, Volume 4, p. 47.

43. "The Voice of the Torah."

44. Op. Cit.

45. I recommend the book *Prayer Walking: Praying On Site With Insight*, by Steve Hawthorne and Graham Kendrick, Creation House, ISBN: 0884192687.

46. Online WWWebster Dictionary.

47. I recommend you read the following books:

"Commentary of the Book of Acts of the Apostles" written by Dr. C. P. Wagner, Volume 3, *Blazing the Way*, Regal Books. ISBN 0-8307-1722-6.

Ephesians: Power and Magic, written by Clinton Arnold, Baker Book House (ISBN 0-8010-2143-X).

Christianizing the Roman Empire, written by Ramsay MacMullen, Yale University Press (ISBN 0-300-03642-6).

48. *The Transforming Power of Revival, Prophetic Strategies into the*

21st Century, edited by Harold Caballeros and Mell Winger, Editorial Peniel, Buenos Aires, Argentina, pp. 14–21 (ISBN 987-9038-24-X).

49. George Otis, Jr. *Spiritual Mapping Research Questions,* Lynnwood, WA, The Sentinel Group, 1997.